D1324414

The GOLDEN DAYS OF GREECE

The
GOLDEN DAYS
OF GREECE

by Olivia Coolidge

ILLUSTRATED BY ENRICO ARNO

THOMAS Y. CROWELL COMPANY   *New York*

93 6
Coo

Designed by Mina Baylis
Manufactured in the United States of America

L.C. Card 68-21599

2   3   4   5   6   7   8   9   10

BY THE AUTHOR:

GREEK MYTHS
LEGENDS OF THE NORTH
THE TROJAN WAR
EGYPTIAN ADVENTURES
CROMWELL'S HEAD
ROMAN PEOPLE
CHURCHILL AND THE STORY OF TWO WORLD WARS
CAESAR'S GALLIC WAR
MEN OF ATHENS
MAKERS OF THE RED REVOLUTION
EDITH WHARTON
PEOPLE IN PALESTINE
LIVES OF THE FAMOUS ROMANS
THE KING OF MEN
EUGENE O'NEILL
WOMEN'S RIGHTS
MARATHON LOOKS ON THE SEA

Contents

Contents

Introduction

H I S T O R Y is about people like ourselves, but people living in different ways or in different times and places. History, however, talks mostly about the big things of life, such as freedom; and it may leave out the small things we think of most of the time. Even when we do learn how boys and girls lived in other days, we are told much about their strange ways and little of their feelings or their fun.

A famous leader of Athens nearly twenty-five hundred years ago once said, "I rule the Athenians, my wife rules me, and my little boy rules my wife." This reminds us that the Athenians, even if they did not often write about it, did have families they loved and little boys they spoiled, just as people do today.

If we remember that saying when we are reading Greek history, we are not likely to find ourselves thinking we are glad we did not live in those days. We shall understand that people like ourselves have been happy in every time and place and have been as fond of their own ways as we are of those we are used to.

As long as we are sure of this, we shall find that the important things of history are interesting, too. Other people have fought for freedom, and gained it, and found it hard to handle when they had it. Other people have tried to think what goodness means and what is the best way to make people good. We see that men's ideas have not always been the same as our own, even though they wanted the same things.

You have to use your imagination to read history; but if you do, it will be strange if you do not like it. History has so many good stories to tell. We hear about men who win glory, have adventures, and become leaders. We all want to do such things ourselves, and it thrills us to hear about the great deeds of other people. There are chances to do fine things in every time and place, so that every age in history has had heroes.

No people ever enjoyed living more than the Greeks did. They have left us good stories and things to think about as well. It is easy to like Greek history, and as Americans we have a special feeling for it. We too call ourselves lovers of freedom, and this makes it natural for us to enjoy the adventures of a free people.

I

The Free Land
and Its People

GREECE is a small, rocky country which looks like the end of an arm thrust into the sea. At the southern end of it dangles a hand on a very thin wrist which is called the Peloponnese, or the Island of Pelops. People are never far from the sea in Greece, so that it is often easier to go by boat from one place to another than to cross the mountains which lie in between. Greeks have always been great sailors, and many of them live on islands.

The tiny sea which lies to the east between Greece and modern Turkey is called the Aegean.

It is dotted all over with islands, so that sailors are hardly ever out of sight of land. This made it easy for Greeks to get about from early times; and soon they built cities all down the Turkish coast of the Aegean, in Asia Minor, as it used to be called. When the Greeks spoke of their country as a whole, they meant not only what we call Greece, but the islands of the Aegean Sea, the land on all its edges, and a few more distant ports as well.

Greece is a poor country, better for goats and donkeys than for horses and cattle. It grows grain in the few places where there is flat land. Its most famous fruits are grapes and olives. Greeks used olive oil for cooking, for lamps, and even for soap. They ate raisins and olives, bread, goat's-milk cheese, and fish, as well as vegetables. They drank wine mixed with water. They lived far more simply than we do, but their lives held plenty of adventures.

Greek houses were small and bare because people were mostly out of doors. Winter is wet and stormy; but when spring comes, the days grow clear. The hillsides are gay with millions of flowers. Summer is warm and cloudless, but not too hot because a wind blows often. The sea and the sky are the brightest possible blue, and the air is so clear that you can see a long way off. Greece is a good land for people who love beauty.

The land belonged to the Greeks as a whole, but its coves and islands were hard to combine into a single state. Every Greek had his home town, which he called his city. This had walls for defense and farmland outside it. If the district was big enough, it had outlying villages too. Each city was free to govern itself, and there were plenty of quarrels between cities, because the Greeks were active people who enjoyed a good fight. But they all spoke the same language, had the same customs, and prayed to the same gods. Some of their great men came from one city or island, some from another. Most of them, however, came from the greatest city of all, the city of Athens.

This need not give you the idea that Greeks are dull to learn about because their world was smaller and poorer than ours. They enjoyed life, and they found things to think about as well as to do. Indeed, the first thing people like about the Greeks is their imagination.

Because they were outdoor people, they wondered often about the workings of nature. One man had a fair voyage, while the next ran into a storm. One year spring rains were right for the crops, but the next was too dry. One man died young, while his brother lived to a good old age. On the whole, the Greeks thought that nature was rather like themselves. People got angry, tired, or careless. Sometimes they felt gay, and sometimes gloomy. In fact, although their lives had a general pattern, men varied a good deal from day to day. This is true of the weather and the growth of things, so that Greeks thought of gods like themselves as ruling nature.

Because the Greek world was so beautiful, it was clear to everyone that the gods must be far more beautiful than men. The Greeks soon gave names to their gods and began to make up stories about them. Zeus was god of the sky and father of all. Poseidon, his brother, was god of the sea. Apollo, god of the sun, drove a shining chariot across the sky every day; while at night Artemis, his twin sister, drove the moon.

All the gods and goddesses had adventures because the Greeks could not imagine beings who did not live interesting lives. Many stories were told not only about the gods, but about heroes of the past who knew the gods far better than people of later days. Typical of these were the adventures of the hero Hercules, who became a god in the end. Hercules killed monsters, traveled to strange lands, and even went down below the earth where the ghosts of the dead live, and came back alive. You can read many stories which the Greeks used to tell about their gods and heroes. Most of them are over three thousand years old, and yet they are still fresh and vivid.

Many of these tales are too long to tell here, but one of the shorter ones is worth picking out because it is about the founding of the city which represents all the finest things in Greece.

Athens lies on the mainland of Greece, a little north of the Peloponnese; and even today it is the capital city of the country. It is built on a fairly flat plain around a huge rock or steep hill called the Acropolis, which was the site of the earliest stronghold and was always a sacred place to the Athenians. From the Acropolis you can see mountains on one hand and islands out to sea on the other; for Athens, though it lies a few miles inland, commands two splendid harbors.

The story says that when this city was founded, the gods in their wisdom saw what a famous place it was going to be. Several gods were eager to become the chief god of Athens, but two of them seemed to have the best claims. The first of these was Poseidon, god of the sea, because the Athenians were to be a seafaring people. The second was Athene, goddess of wisdom and of household arts. It was agreed that the one who gave the new city the best gift should have the honor.

The gods came down onto the Acropolis and asked Cecrops, first king of Athens, to be their judge. Then Poseidon, who was a stately elder god with long hair and beard, both blue, struck the ground with the trident or three-pronged spear which he used to guide his horses over the tops of the waves. You can still see the white manes of Poseidon's horses tossing on the waves when the wind is strong. At Poseidon's blow, the earth quaked and split open. Out of the gap bounded a splendid white horse, and where his hoof first hit the rock, a stream of salt water gushed forth. All admired Poseidon's gift, for horses were scarce in Greece, and none so fine had ever been seen.

Athene, however, did nothing exciting. Athene was a beautiful young girl in a long white robe. She had armor and was a great fighter when she was needed, but for the moment she was not concerned with war. She bent down and fumbled in the dust. Between her hands there grew up an ugly little tree, small and dusty, with gray-green leaves and little hard green berries.

The gods began to smile, but Athene explained that this was the olive, which would give people food and fuel and soap. The Athenians would grow rich from selling their olive oil, and

she would teach them how to make the jars in which it was stored, things of beauty and value. In fact, the olive would make Athens great in trade and many useful arts.

Needless to say, Athene won the contest. As a result, if you go to Athens today, you will see on the Acropolis the ruins of one of the most beautiful buildings in the world. It is the Parthenon, or Temple of the Maiden, sacred to the maiden goddess Athene, who gave the olive tree to her own city.

II

A Tale of
Buried Treasure
1900–1200 B.C.

A STUDENT of history is often like a good detective. Much of the distant past is lost, but by following up clues a man may discover the remains of a great age. It is a thrilling moment when he finds its treasures.

A hundred years ago we knew little about the early Greeks, partly because we did not believe all that the later ones told us. The general outline of history was clear enough, but we could not tell much about how people lived in those days and what went on.

In the beginning, the Greeks were a wandering people who entered their country from the north, where it joins the rest of Europe. They came in two main waves, hundreds of years apart. The first group, which we now think arrived about 1900 B.C., called themselves Achaeans. They used weapons and tools of bronze, which is a mixture of copper and tin. It held a sharp edge quite well, but it had the drawback that tin was hard to come by.

The rule of these Achaeans was broken up by the Dorians, who arrived about seven hundred years later. The Dorians had learned to use iron, which is more common than tin. They had many more weapons and tools, so that a new way of life began to grow up. This brought us down to times about which we know more.

The big question was what had happened during those seven hundred years when the Achaeans with their bronze tools ruled the land. The later Greeks thought they knew a good deal about those times because they had stories and poems to tell them. *The Iliad* of Homer gives us part of the tale of how King Agamemnon of Mycenae in the Peloponnese got the other kings and heroes of Greece to help him take King Priam's city of Troy in Asia Minor. *The Odyssey* is the story of a voyage of the hero Odysseus all around the Mediterranean Sea. It gives a picture of what the world was thought to be like and how its people lived. No wonder that the Greeks felt they knew the days of the Achaeans.

The Iliad and *The Odyssey* are splendid poems, among the most famous in the world. They tell us what the Achaeans looked like, how they lived, what they felt about life. All the same, let us stop to ask who Homer was and what he really knew about the Achaeans.

A Tale of Buried Treasure, 1900–1200 B. C.

The later Greeks say that Homer was a blind minstrel who came from one of the Greek cities in Asia Minor. A minstrel was a wandering story-teller who chanted his poems while playing on a small harp called a lyre. He had learned his trade, ever since he was a small boy, by acting as servant to a minstrel and listening to his poems until he knew them by heart. Soon he grew eager to pick up songs from other minstrels, too. When he became a minstrel himself, he combined or added to the stories he knew, changing them as suited him. In his turn he taught these to the boy who traveled with him. At last, between four and five hundred years after the end of the Achaean age, a very great minstrel (or perhaps two, as some people think) shaped *The Iliad* and *The Odyssey* as we know them.

Have you ever played a game in which one person whispers a sentence into his neighbor's ear? He whispers what he heard to the next person, and so on all down the row. At the end of it you find that what the last one heard is quite different from the sentence which the first one spoke in the beginning. *The Iliad* and *The Odyssey,* many thought, were like the result of this game. They told us a good deal about the times of the minstrels, but very little about the age of the Achaeans when the stories had started. In fact, scholars said there never was a Trojan War or a King Agamemnon.

A little boy of seven called Heinrich Schliemann got a book from his father for Christmas in 1822. It was a book of historical tales and legends, and in it was a picture of Troy burning when it was taken by King Agamemnon. Little Heinrich wanted to know if that was what Troy looked like and if it was true, as the book said, that Troy had vanished so that nobody knew where it had been. That was true, the father said. All the riches and glory of King Agamemnon had disappeared, too.

"When I am big," Heinrich Schliemann said, "I shall go to Greece and find Troy and the king's treasure."

The Schliemanns were poor people, so that Heinrich left school at fourteen to become a grocer's boy in a small north German town near where he was born. But he was clever and worked hard. He was lucky and adventurous, too. Soon he signed on in a ship as cabin boy. After that he went to many places, learned many languages, and became a rich banker and merchant. But he never forgot his wish to find Troy.

He knew that the scholars said there had never been a siege of Troy or a King Agamemnon, but he did not believe them. When he was forty-five, he gave up his business and went to find Troy. At least people agreed that such a city had once existed.

Everyone knew where "New Troy" had been. The Romans had built it on a hillock now called the mound of Hissarlik, a little inland from the coast of Asia Minor. But people thought old Troy had been somewhere else. Schliemann checked what Homer said about the land around Troy, and especially about the springs from which the people drew water. He decided that Hissarlik was the right place after all. He hired laborers and started to dig.

All the experts said he was a fool. The laborers cheated him. The Turkish rulers of those parts were unfriendly. The spot was unhealthy, and the drinking water was bad. Schliemann was not to be put off. In the short season when it was not too hot or too wet he dug there for four summers. Presently he was discovering strange things.

The Roman city of New Troy had been built on top of the ruins of an earlier town, which in turn was on top of another earlier yet. As Schliemann dug deeper and deeper, he found nine cities, each earlier than the last. Indeed, the bottom layer was so ancient that its people had not yet learned how to use metals.

The most thrilling thing to Schliemann was that the second and third lowest levels had been destroyed by fire, as Homer's Troy had been. Schliemann found huge walls and a ruined gate buried in ashes which he thought must be the palace of King Priam and the great gate of the city which Homer speaks of.

Excited though he was, he decided in 1873 to

go to Greece. On the day before the workmen were to stop digging, Schliemann was down at the bottom of a pit twenty-eight feet deep near the foot of "Priam's Palace" when he saw a gleam of gold in the turned earth.

"Quick!" he whispered to his wife. "Send the men home!" He was afraid that they might steal anything of value.

His wife, who was a Greek and spoke Turkish to the men, did not know what to say. He told her to tell them that it was his birthday, and they could have the rest of the day off. As soon as they had gone, he went to work with his own knife, scraping under the great stone blocks of the wall, which might easily have crashed on top of him. His wife spread her red shawl on the ground, and on it they piled the treasure of a king—crowns, brooches, bracelets, and other jewelry of gold which had been buried, packed in boxes, amid the ruins of the "house of Priam." So, at least, Schliemann thought. It was the greatest moment of his life so far. But even more wonderful things were soon to come.

A Tale of Buried Treasure, 1900–1200 B.C.

Mycenae lies in the Peloponnese on a rocky hill looking over one of the fairest plains in Greece. Some of the ruins of the old walls were still to be seen, while a traveler in Roman times had said that the graves of Agamemnon and his family were there. Schliemann was eager to find them.

He discovered not the graves of Homer's heroes, but the treasures of a lost age. He found ornaments in the shape of animals, flowers, and fish. There were pictures of warriors fighting or hunting lions and deer. There were gold masks, showing the actual features of dead kings. Suddenly the Bronze Age of the Achaeans leaped into life, so that for the first time we could begin to tell how far Homer describes them as they lived.

Ever since that time people have been digging, not only in Troy and Mycenae, but in other places which Homer spoke of. They are patient, careful people who go more slowly than Schliemann did because we know now that in his haste he destroyed some things we should have liked to look at. By now we have many more treasures of the Bronze Age than Schliemann found. We can even see that Homer knew a good deal. For instance, in *The Odyssey* Odysseus' son goes to visit an old king called Nestor, who gives him a drink out of a famous cup with doves on the handles. A cup of this kind has been found; and though it is not quite the same, still we can see that Homer was speaking of one like it.

We know a great deal about the men of Mycenae today. They were dark-haired, slender, sharp-featured men, fond of war and hunting, but traders and craftsmen as well. Their king was not only a leader in war; he was the center of everything that went on. He had his clerks to keep his accounts, his craftsmen to make his weapons and tools, his farmers to fill the storerooms with grain and oil. His donkeys and porters carried the wares down to his ships, and across the sea his traders had their ports where they sold his goods. All this belonged to the king, because his people needed him to keep them together. Everybody worked at his own trade and generally trained his sons to come after him. The king was rich, while many were poor; but they were proud of his fine robes and jewels. They thought his prayers brought better luck than their own because he was a hero whom the gods loved.

Agamemnon's palace can be seen today in outline, its foundations uncovered. It is thrilling to stand by his great hearth, to look out from his terrace onto the plain, or to sit down in his guest room. The stories we hear about him from Homer fit in well with what has been discovered in Mycenae. By now we are beginning to be able to read the king's accounts, which were kept on tablets of clay. They are written in Greek, but the letters are different from those of later times. King Agamemnon and many earlier kings are quite well known to us today. We have taken a step back into the past of a famous people. All this came about because a boy of seven said to himself one Christmas, "I'll go and find Troy and the king's treasure."

III

Look Before You Leap
546 B.C.

W H E N the Dorians with their iron swords swept over Greece about 1200 B.C., they came by land and sea from the north. Some lucky cities like Athens were never conquered. After burning others, the Dorians wandered on. In yet other places, mostly in the Peloponnese, which is the southern part of Greece, they settled down.

Many years were needed before the Dorians and the earlier Greeks forgot their differences and began to think of themselves as one people. Meanwhile, Greeks from the mainland, both Dorians and others, spread over the islands and coasts of the Aegean Sea. Some of their cities in Asia Minor traded with wealthy kingdoms inland and grew very great. Through them, Greek ways began to be known to their neighbors.

Croesus, the richest man in his world, ruled over one of these kingdoms in Asia Minor during the middle of the sixth century B.C. He knew the Greeks well and was pleased to have a visit from Solon of Athens, who was one of the wisest men alive.

Solon had been asked by the Athenians to draw up for them a new set of laws which would be fairer than those of the past. He had done what they asked; but since he did not wish to be dictator, he had gone away to let the Athenians try out the new laws for themselves.

Croesus greeted him with great honor. He showed him his great palace, his gold treasure, his fine robes and splendid furnishings, his jewels, and everything which he owned. Then with a smile of pride, he asked Solon who was the happiest man in the world.

"Tellus of Athens, sire," replied Solon.

Amazed and angry, Croesus asked why.

"First, because his country flourished in his days and he himself had sons both beautiful and good. He lived to see children born to each of them, and these children all grew up. Further, because after a life spent in what our people look on as comfort, his end was glorious. In a battle between Athenians and their neighbors he came to the aid of his countrymen, put the foe to flight, and died bravely on the field. The Athenians gave him a public funeral where he fell and paid him the highest honors."

Croesus did not see why a man should be called happy just because his country had been lucky, because his family had been good, and because he had died gloriously. All the same, he asked the question again, thinking he might be given second place. But Solon told him that Cleobis and Bito were the next happiest.

Cleobis and Bito, Solon said, were two youths of Argos who behaved so nobly to their mother that she prayed the gods to give them their best gift. Next day the two fell asleep in the pride of their youth and so died without having known sorrow. The Argives put up statues in their honor.

Solon, it seemed, was praising poorer men than Croesus, men who were never counted happy until life was over, and men who cared greatly about honor. Croesus parted from Solon in anger, but he did not quite forget what he had been told.

Years passed, and a warrior king called Cyrus arose in Persia, which was over two months' journey away, beyond the Tigris and near the borders of the Red Sea. One might think that Croesus would have been safe from the Persian, seeing that there were mighty empires between the two countries. Presently, however, these were overthrown. The empire of the Persian spread as far as Asia Minor to the very edge of Croesus' kingdom.

Croesus was not sure what he ought to do. Should he wait and hope that Cyrus would leave him alone, or should he attack before his rival was ready? He thought it best to take advice;

and so he sent to ask the Greek oracle at Delphi.

The temple of Apollo at Delphi is in one of the most beautiful spots in Greece, high up on the slope of a hill with a view of mountains across a narrow valley which runs down to the sea. Amid all the quarrels which the Greek cities had with one another, they all worshiped at this famous temple, whose priests often acted as umpires.

Apollo was the god who foretold the future,

and his oracle at Delphi was a place where people came to ask him questions about things they wanted to know. They put these questions to the priests of the temple, who in turn repeated them to Apollo's priestess. She took her seat on a three-legged bowl placed over a deep crack in the earth. We do not know whether some gas came out of this crack, or whether the priestess chewed special drugs. At all events, she went into a strange fit in which she shrieked out words or sentences which often did not make sense. It was up to the priests to guess her meaning and give a proper answer to the inquiry.

It is easy to say that this was a fraud by which the priests deceived the people, but in fact things were not as simple as that. Everyone expected the priests to use their heads in figuring out what Apollo's priestess must have meant. Besides, the god was not supposed to give straight answers. If you went to Delphi and asked, "Who stole my red cow?" you were not going to get a simple name in reply. Apollo might curse the cow-stealer in a way which would frighten him into giving it back. Or he might answer in a riddle which you had to guess before you were any wiser.

Often the problems which came to Apollo at Delphi were not questions at all. People or cities complained of one another for breaking agreements or sacred laws. Apollo, by cursing the offender, forced him to behave better. In this way the temple at Delphi helped to unite the tiny states under common rules of conduct.

King Croesus sent to ask the advice of Apollo; and because he was a very rich king, he gave great gifts. He sent a gold statue of a lion, two huge bowls made of gold and silver, four silver casks, several other gold and silver vessels, the gold statue of a woman, and some of the jewelry of his wife. (She had plenty more.) Giving these, he asked whether he should go to war with the Persians.

The priests of Apollo were clever at such questions; and they answered that if Croesus did so, he would destroy a great empire. Thus encouraged, he attacked. Alas, the great empire which

was destroyed soon proved to be his own. Apollo had been careful to be right either way.

These stories about Croesus and the Greeks are told us by the Greek historian Herodotos, who was a fine collector of good stories. He adds that when the Persian king Cyrus was about to put Croesus to death, he heard the old man call on Solon and asked why. Then Croesus told him how Solon had said that no man could be counted as happy until he was dead. Cyrus was impressed by this wisdom. He forgave Croesus and made him one of his advisers.

These tales are probably not all true, but they show us history. Solon and Croesus were real people. Real also is the contrast between the Greek idea of a good life and the splendor of the great Asian kingdoms. Greeks knew that life was hard for many, and they were content if they had good health, good children, good neighbors, and good luck. They wanted to be citizens whose memory was kept alive, even after death, by their own people. They did not think that great wealth made men happy, and they were not impressed by kings.

All this made it difficult for Greeks to get along with Asiatics, who looked on their kings and their nobles as godlike men, born to rule over other people. For this reason it is important to notice that when Croesus had been conquered, Greek cities on the coast of Asia Minor found themselves next to an empire of the hugest size that had ever been seen. The son of Cyrus conquered Egypt. The third king, Darius, who was the greatest of all, ruled an empire which stretched right out to the north of India. A question for the future was how the Greeks could defend their freedom against these mighty Persians.

IV

The Olympic Games
776 B.C.– A.D. 393

THE ORACLE at Delphi helped Greeks to feel that they belonged to one family. More important still in this way were the athletic games which took place in several parts of Greece. The greatest among these were the Olympic games in honor of Zeus, which were held at Olympia in the territory of Elis, a city of the Peloponnese. These Olympic festivals came every four years, and the period between one and the next was called an Olympiad. It was by Olympiads that all the Greeks reckoned dates, so that, for instance, 701 B.C. would be the fourth year of the nineteenth Olympiad. This shows how important the Olympics were to every city.

A year before the games, the men of Elis, which was the city in charge of them, sent messengers through Greece to proclaim that the sacred year of the games was just beginning. This was the signal for all the best athletes to go into special training. Let us follow the fortunes of an Athenian runner who was called Pheidippides.

Athletics had started for Pheidippides when he was about seven years old and went to school. He was not a baby now, so his father gave him a tutor, an older servant who went about with him everywhere and even slept in the same room. The Greeks did not believe in allowing boys to be naughty, and they saw to it that a child was never out of sight of somebody whose duty it was to teach him to behave. Pheidippides had to keep himself tidy, wear his cloak drawn tightly about him, keep his eyes on the ground in the presence of older people, and never speak until he was spoken to. It must have been very boring. Luckily for him, he was busy most of the day.

Early in the morning his tutor took him to school and sat watching while he learned in company with other boys to read and write and to recite Homer. The schoolmaster had a stick or a strap which he used if Pheidippides did not pay close attention. The boy spent many hours on these studies, for the Greeks thought that Homer taught history, poetry, and sacred studies as well as respect for virtue. Pheidippides, however, had music lessons as well, where he practiced singing or learned to play the lyre.

At the end of a long morning, we can imagine how a boy needed to run about after having such close watch kept on him. For Pheidippides, the best moment of the day must have been the one when he went out to the exercise grounds with his tutor, who carried a little oil flask and scraper for him to use later. Here the boys ran foot races, threw javelins, or cast the discus, which was thrown with an underarm swing. They practiced the long jump or wrestled. Some learned how to box, covering their hands with heavy leather straps which did far more damage than our padded boxing gloves today; but many of the Greeks did not care for boxing. They were tough in war, but they did not much like brutal sports.

Pheidippides, who was not very rich, would not often get a chance to practice chariot racing. This was always a rich man's sport, as horse racing is today. The owner of the horses counted as the winner, while his driver, like a modern jockey, was only the man whom he hired to win his race.

It was hot and dusty in the exercise ground, and Pheidippides practiced naked. There is a story told that in the early days of Olympia all the athletes had to wear loincloths. One young man who thought he could run faster without it arranged his garment so that it fell off. He won the race, and the umpires did not know what to do about it. At last they agreed that no one need wear anything.

By the time he had finished practicing, the

boy was dusty and sweaty. Before he put on his clothes again, he smeared himself all over with olive oil out of the little jar his tutor carried. Then he scraped the oil off, taking with it the dirt and sweat from his body. This was not as pleasant as a shower, but it was a pretty good way of getting clean in a hot country where water runs short in the summer.

Athens had athletic meets of its own, so that Pheidippides soon had a chance to run in the boys' games which were held in honor of Theseus. He must have won these, and when school-days were behind him, he went on practicing with other young men. The Athenians had regular games for young men, too; and every few years they had special games in honor of Athene.

The result of this was that by the time Pheidippides was ready to train for Olympia, everyone in Athens knew just how good a runner he was and felt nearly as eager for him to win as he did himself.

Eleven months went quickly by, and all the athletes had to go down to Elis for the last month. Their trainers went with them, together with servants carrying food and supplies of all sorts. Athens was a great city, so that it surely would have a good number of young men entering for different events. The city would be proud to send out the Athenian party looking gay and well equipped so that it would make a good show when it passed through other cities on its way to Olympia.

While Pheidippides was having his last training in Elis and getting to know the young men who were running against him, more messengers went out through all the cities proclaiming a sacred truce. This meant that if there was a war going on, as there too often was, it must be halted to let people travel to the great games and get back home. Among the early Greeks this truce was certainly kept, but later it was sometimes broken, as people became less afraid than they once had been of the curses of Zeus.

At last the great day came, and the chief men of Elis led all the athletes in a splendid procession out of the city to Olympia, where the games were held. It is difficult to describe this because in early Greece it was an open field, merely more level than most Greek fields. Even later on, the stadium was not as huge as some of the Roman ones or as the football stadiums we are used to. It was long and narrow, and people crowded on the sidelines to watch. Nearby there was a beautiful temple of Zeus, together with other temples and buildings. All around, there would be wooden booths of every sort, for the games at Olympia were a great fair and market as well.

Vast crowds came to watch the games. It was easy to sleep out of doors in fine August weather, and many people had brought simple meals with them. In any case, there was plenty of food being sold, as well as goods of every sort, both useful and strange or costly. It would be amazing also to see what other things were going on. A poet might be giving a reading of his works, to which people listened as you might to a concert. This was his way of getting known, and it might easily be your only chance of hearing his poems.

In the same way, a learned man might be

giving a lecture on how the world was made of atoms, or what the customs of the Egyptians were like, or how to cure fevers. People would flock to listen because Greeks were always eager to pick up new ideas. All the same, if you did not feel in a mood for this, there would be acrobats and jugglers to amuse you. All around you people would be greeting friends whom they had not met for years, since everybody seemed to turn up at the games.

While all this was going on, Pheidippides and his friends would be making sacrifices to the gods. Nobody ever forgot for a moment that the Olympics were more than an athletic meet. They were held in praise of Zeus, in whose honor each young man killed an animal. The insides were burned on the altar of the god. The rest made a feast for their friends, though they themselves were not allowed to eat by the rules of their training. The prayers, sacrifices, and feasts made this Zeus's special day, while the excitements of the fair kept everyone happy.

The next three days were for sports, and the

final one was for prize-giving. Pheidippides must have won, because he became the most famous runner in Greece. On the fifth and last day he would get his prize, which was nothing more than a ribbon to bind his hair and a crown of wild olive. The Athenians would go mad with cheering him. Perhaps some famous artist would be hired to make a statue of him to put up at Olympia. It was even possible that the Athenians would put one up when he got home. A poem might be written to him. We have a number of poems written by the famous poet Pindar

for victors in the Pythian games, which were held at Delphi for Apollo.

The Athenians would go home in triumph with Pheidippides in their midst, showing off in every town along the way. When he got back, the heads of the state would come out of the city to meet him. They would take him to the temple of Athene, where he would hang his crown of olive. Presents would come pouring in. He would get a prize in money. All his life he would have a front seat on great occasions, and he could dine every day at the City Hall, where the magistrates, foreign envoys, or great men were fed by the public. Pheidippides had brought great honor to his city.

Today our Olympic games imitate these famous games of Greece, where sport, at least for a short while, took the place of war. Our athletics are more varied, but we try to keep up the same customs. There is one big difference, however. Are you wondering what happened in the women's events at Olympia? There never were any. Greek women married at about fourteen, and they were hardly ever seen outside their homes. If you wanted to enjoy fun or have adventures in Greece, you nearly always had to be born a boy.

V

Aristodemos
the Spartan

about 500–479 B.C.

MOST famous of the Dorians who settled in the Peloponnese were the ones who lived in Sparta. Unlike most places in Greece, Sparta lies inland on a wide plain which is ringed with mountains. It was a country that needed good soldiers to defend it, because unless the Spartans were masters of these mountains, they could be raided from them. As long as they were so, it was easy to protect themselves from their neighbors.

When the Dorians had seized the Spartan plain, they had found it thickly settled, because flat land for farming was not common in Greece. Instead of killing the people who lived there, the Dorians made them servants, almost slaves. They themselves were fighting men, and they wanted workers to support them. This divided the people of the Spartan land into two groups who did not, as time went on, grow together. The Spartans, as the Dorians liked to call themselves, were few in number. In order to remain masters, they organized themselves in a special way. How this worked out, we may see from the case of Aristodemos, who was born in Sparta not long after Pheidippides was born in Athens.

For the first seven years of their lives there would not have been much difference between the two boys, except that Aristodemos might be rougher. He lived with his mother, did not see much of his father, wore no clothes at all when it was hot, had a few toys, and played with the other boys some of the games which boys play now.

At seven years old, both boys were no longer babies. Pheidippides got a tutor to teach him good manners, and he went to school. Aristodemos left his mother and went to live in barracks with other boys. Here he simply learned to be tough. He was only allowed one garment, a sleeveless tunic, for summer or winter, no matter how cold it was. He slept on the floor on reeds which he cut himself. He was always hungry because he was not given enough to eat, so that he had to steal some of his food. The Spartans thought this practice in looking after himself would be useful when he went to war. If Aristodemos was caught stealing, he was severely beaten for being clumsy enough to be found out.

He was always being beaten for one thing or another. He belonged to a company which had at the head of it one or two of the young men. It was their duty to teach the little boys to bear pain without crying out, and you may be sure they did so. They showed them how to use weapons as well, took them on long marches, and so forth. Aristodemos did practice some of the athletics which Pheidippides was enjoying at Athens, but on the whole the Spartans liked sports which would be useful in war, like running in full armor or the brutal boxing, which was really unarmed combat.

Aristodemos learned to read and write because messages have to be sent in war. He did not spend much time on this, and he was not allowed to read often or to listen to lectures. He learned not to chatter, but to express his opinions briefly and bluntly.

He did not hate all this as much as you would do, because he made good friends and was proud of his toughness. When he grew too old for the boys' barracks, he simply moved into one for the young men.

He never did any useful work. Every Spartan family owned a certain number of farms. The people who lived on these were called a man's Helots and were almost his slaves. They were the conquered peoples who had been living on the land when the Spartans had arrived. Every month, his Helots had to provide a fixed ration to the mess hall where Aristodemos ate with his friends. One of them became his body servant and went to war with him, carrying his helmet and heavy armor on the march. When food came to be served out to the army, Aristodemos got twice as much as his Helot. We can only hope that he shared part of it sometimes.

Since Aristodemos did not need to earn his living, the state was able to take up all his time. If there was fighting, he went to war under one of the Spartan kings. There were two kings in Sparta, but these were not really rulers so much as commanders in chief. Most of what Aristodemos did when he was not fighting was directed by a council of elders. He served, for instance, on garrison duty in the hills at the edge of the Spartan plain. He made raids on any of the Helots who were suspected of wanting their freedom. A great deal of his time was spent in keeping fit. Spartans did not trade or use money, so that there was no business to be done. Their clothes and armor were made by their women, their Helots, and other subjects who paid them tribute. Sparta itself was a poor village without

any of the fine public buildings of which the Athenians were growing proud.

Fairly soon after he grew up, Aristodemos got married. He thought it his duty to have plenty of sons. But he did not go and live with his wife. Indeed, for a number of years he would have to visit her in secret, just as he had to steal his food when he was younger. Only as he became middle-aged might a man move into his home, and even then he generally ate in the mess hall.

It was really no wonder that the Spartans became the best soldiers in Greece. They were not greatly loved by their neighbors, but people who lived farther off, like the Athenians, could not help admiring them. They might be stupid, but at least they said what they thought. They ate and dressed simply and had few wants, but they spent their lives serving the state. The Athenians, who were so proud of their own city, liked the Spartans for doing their duty.

After King Croesus had been beaten by the Persians, the Greek cities of Asia Minor were soon attacked. They sent for help to the Athenians and the Spartans. The Athenians gave a little, but the Spartans would not fight so far from home. The Greek cities were conquered, and their warships became part of the fleet of the Persians.

More years went by, and the warlike kings of Persia began to think of conquering the Greek mainland also. Both Aristodemos and Pheidippides were going to have to fight for their freedom. The little cities which were so jealous of one another needed to combine under a leader. It was only natural that all looked to the Spartans, who were the best fighters.

VI

The Persians Attack
490–479 B.C.

THE ATTACK of the Persians on Greece was not long in coming. In 490 B.C., King Darius sent a fleet to conquer some of the islands and then go on to attack the Athenians. The Athenians sent to the Spartans for help. But when the enemy appeared in plain sight, sailing for the bay of Marathon twenty miles from Athens, the Spartans were still a hundred and fifty miles away in their homeland.

There were no good roads in Greece, and the mountains were too steep for a rider on horseback. Now was the time for Pheidippides, the fastest runner in Greece, to aid his country. He covered the hills between Athens and Sparta in two days, or so it is said. No modern runner has ever tried this feat, yet people think Pheidippides may really have done it for his city.

Despite his effort, the Spartans did not set out to the rescue. It happened to be a sacred month with them, so that they waited till the new moon lest they offend their gods. It may be that they did not greatly care what happened to Athens as long as they were safe in the Peloponnese.

Luckily the Athenians had a great general called Miltiades, who saw a chance to take the Persians by surprise. Falling on them like a thunderbolt, Miltiades drove them back to their ships with heavy losses. By the battle of Marathon, the Athenians saved themselves without Spartan help. Afterwards Miltiades gave the helmet which he had worn on that glorious day to the temple of Zeus in Olympia. There it was found not many years ago by one of the patient diggers who have been working in Greece ever since the days of Schliemann. If you ever visit

Greece, you can see this helmet, which was worn by the famous Athenian who saved his country.

A few years later, King Darius of Persia died and was succeeded by his son Xerxes. The new king wanted to show that he was as good a man as his father, and so he decided to invade Greece at the head of his armies. He sent messengers through his empire to collect them.

The best of Xerxes's soldiers were a picked group of guards, ten thousand in number, who were called the Immortals because as soon as any man was killed another was waiting to make up the number. These were foot soldiers armed with spears, but Xerxes had splendid cavalry and many archers as well. Besides these, he had other spearmen nearly as good who were either Persian or from kindred peoples. They all wore lighter armor than the Greeks, but they did not think much of Greek armies, as long as they could break up the force of their charge by using archers.

King Xerxes had a huge empire, and every part of it was forced to send him fighters. He had warriors of every kind. There were black men in leopard skins from Ethiopia carrying flint-tipped weapons because they did not know how to use metals. There were yellow-skinned, slant-eyed men with strange headdresses made out of the scalps of horses with manes and ears left on them. There were brown men from India in cotton robes, with bows and arrows of bamboo. Men rode in chariots, on ponies, donkeys, or camels. They had helmets or armor of skins, wood, metal, plaited straw, or padded linen. Their weapons varied from pointed stakes or clubs to darts, lassos, and arrows. A great many of these strange people can have been of little use to Xerxes in battle, but they looked fierce and could be used in foraging for supplies. Besides, when they went back home, they would tell their friends how great was the power of the Persian king.

This army came together early in 480 B.C. in Sardis of Asia Minor, which had been the capital of King Croesus. No one was allowed to make excuses. One rich man asked if the eldest of his five sons might stay at home, since all the rest were with the army. Xerxes had the young man slain at once. Half of his body was placed on either side of the great gate of Sardis, out of which the army marched. Xerxes himself rode with them in a chariot. In front of him went an empty chariot drawn by white horses as a symbol that the unseen god of the Persians was going to war.

The army marched to the narrow channel which divides Asia Minor from Europe in the northeast corner of the Aegean. This strait, which was called the Hellespont, connects the Black Sea with the Aegean. It is about a mile wide at its narrowest part and has a strong current like a swift river. Xerxes had ordered his fleet to meet him here, and it was busy making a bridge of boats for the army to cross.

Men had fastened thick ropes across the strait and were trying to lay ships side by side so that they could make a road across them. This was not easy because of the current, and presently a storm broke the bridge apart before it was ready.

Xerxes ordered his men to lash the waters with chains in order to show the spirits which dwelt in them that the Great King was angry. To show the same thing to the army, he ordered that those in charge of the work should lose their lives. On their second try, the engineers had better luck. Xerxes made offerings and said prayers; then the army started to cross. Herodotos, the historian, says that it took them seven days and nights to do so.

While this vast army crossed into Europe and began to make its way around the coast of the Aegean and into the north of Greece, all the cities were in a panic. Those nearest the Persians hastened to submit; but those farther south, like the Athenians and Spartans, were eager to resist. The army of King Xerxes was keeping near the sea because his fleet, which was carrying some of his supplies, was sailing down the coast. It so happened that the coast road went through a narrow place called the pass of Thermopylae, where the mountains ran close to the sea. It was a perfect spot for a small army to stop a larger one. What made it even better was that the Persian fleet could not land down the coast behind the Greeks, since this was protected by a long and jagged island.

The Spartans were having more trouble with the calendar. It was an Olympic year and the time of the sacred truce. Besides, they had an important feast of their own. In any case, it seems likely that they wanted to fight farther south. But they could not quite resist the urging of the Athenians, since these formed the greater part of the fleet. Thus the Spartans sent a picked group of three hundred under one of their two kings, Leonidas, to hold the pass of Thermopylae with local forces until their festival was safely over.

Leonidas, who saw that there might be hard fighting, took with him only men who had sons to carry on their families. Among these was Aristodemos. Spartans always went gaily to war. "Come back with your shield or on it," people called after them as they marched out. This was an old Spartan farewell, meaning, "Come back victorious or dead." A beaten man threw away his shield in order to run faster, while a dead man was carried home on his shield by his comrades.

Xerxes with his huge army was in no hurry. By the time that he came in sight of the pass of Thermopylae, Leonidas was already there with his three hundred, plus six thousand other troops under his command. Aristodemos and a friend had caught an eye infection. At this moment they were almost blind, so that Leonidas left them out of range of the fighting.

For two days the Persians battered at the pass of Thermopylae. Even their rain of arrows, even the charge of the Immortals, did not break the resistance of the Greeks, who were partly protected by the cliffs coming down to the road. The Persians were trying to find a way around, but most of the tracks over the mountains were too steep. Leonidas had placed a thousand men to guard these mountain paths. On the second evening, however, a native revealed that there was a possible road. Pushing up this with strong forces during the night, the Persians easily put to flight the Greeks on the mountains and began to descend to the coast behind Thermopylae.

The pass was lost, and messengers told Leonidas that he must retreat before the road was blocked behind him. It seems there was not time for all to get away. Leonidas sent most of his forces off; but he remained to hold up pursuit by a fight to the death. "Have a good breakfast, men," he told his Spartans. "You'll dine in the land of the dead."

They had their good breakfast; and while Xerxes was waiting for their retreat to be blocked before he attacked, they combed their long hair, polished their armor, and brushed their scarlet cloaks so that they should look well in death. Then they fought to the last man, slaying many noble Persians, including two of the brothers of King Xerxes. Some of the other Greeks surrendered, but none of the Spartans. The only man who came home alive was Aristodemos. Even his blinded friend had forced a Helot to guide him up the road toward the battle. When Aristodemos did get back to Sparta, nobody would speak to him for the rest of his life. The poor man had not really been a coward, and, as we shall see, he had a chance to prove himself later.

The pass of Thermopylae was lost; but after the war was over, the Greeks put up a memorial to its brave defenders. On it were carved the words of a famous poet which said as simply as the Spartans themselves might have done:

"Go tell the Spartans, thou who passest by,
That here, obedient to their word, we lie."

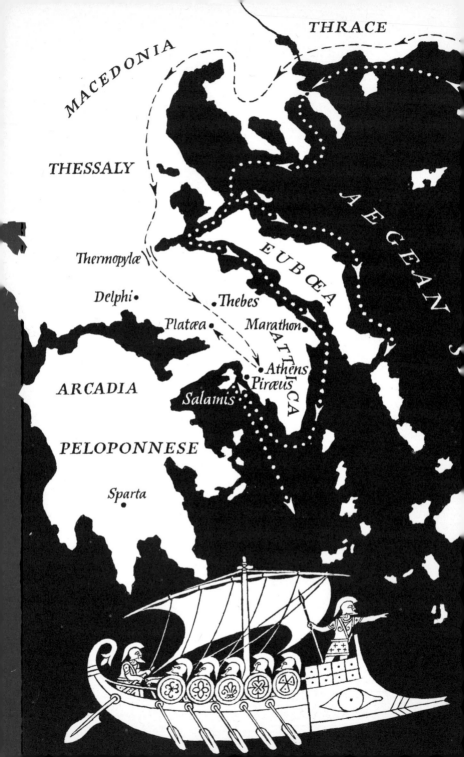

Hellespont

MYSIA

Hermus R.
Sardis

LYDIA

— — — — —► *Xerxes' army*
· · · · · · · · · ·► *the Persian fleet*

Persian Invasion of Greece

VII

The Greek Victories

480–479 B.C.

NOT LONG before the Persian attack, the Athenians had discovered silver mines in their land. The state found itself rich, and a suggestion was made that every citizen should get a bonus. Luckily for the Athenians, they had a leader called Themistocles, who advised them to put the money into building warships. By the beginning of the war they had two hundred, nearly as many as the rest of the Greeks put together.

Greek warships, usually called triremes, were about a hundred and twenty feet long and fifteen wide. They had a crew of two hundred rowers so closely crowded that they had to go ashore to cook or sleep. Each ship carried about a dozen armed men, but its chief weapon was a pointed metal beak below the waterline which would crash through the timbers of an enemy, especially if it were rammed in the side. You can see that the trireme needed skilled rowers and helmsmen.

When the pass of Thermopylae was lost, there was nowhere to stop Xerxes's army before the neck of land or isthmus which joins the Peloponnese to the rest of Greece. The Athenians asked the oracle at Delphi what they should do and were ordered in words they did not understand to put their trust in wooden walls. Themistocles told the people that these "walls" were their wooden ships. The Athenians took to their ships, moving their goats, women, children, and old men to parts of the Peloponnese or to the island of Salamis. This lay opposite Athens, sheltering a largish bay and marking narrow entrances to it at either end.

In this bay Themistocles desired to fight a battle. At the isthmus, where the Spartans wanted to make their stand, there was no good place to trap the Persian fleet. Crowded into the narrow waters of Salamis Bay, it might be defeated.

Xerxes arrived to find Athens empty. He burned it to the ground and sent his men out to plunder. His fleet, arriving at the eastern end of the bay of Salamis, anchored there, unwilling to enter.

The Greeks, inside the western end of the same bay, were still arguing about what to do. Themistocles, who found that he could not get the Spartan general to hold his ground, decided on a trick. He sent secretly to the Persians a trusted servant called Sicinnus, who was tutor to his children. Sicinnus was to say that Themistocles was in despair and had decided to turn traitor. The Greeks were going to escape at dawn. Let the Persians send ships around outside the island of Salamis and block their exit.

Then the main fleet could charge across Salamis Bay to catch the Greeks in the rear as they tried to get out.

The Persians took his advice and blocked the exit; but when the Greeks knew they had to fight, they were ready to fall in with the rest of Themistocles' plan. Very early in the morning they drew up their ships in line. They had about three hundred, but nearly a third of them were turned to face the other way. As the men took their places, they were singing a hymn which they all knew.

Xerxes had a throne set up on shore in a spot from which he could see the whole battle. He took his seat on it, with his guards and secretaries beside him, knowing that his men would fight their best under his own eye.

The Persians entered Salamis Bay in a column because they had to pass through the narrows to get in. The result was that they were in a bad position when the Greek warships which they had thought were running away came charging at them. They were forced into a dense mass as those in front were halted, while those behind came pushing on to get into the battle. Ships collided; oars were broken; vessels were packed too close to move. Many of the Persians fought bravely, but they had no room to turn and face the sharp beaks of the Greek triremes.

A fresh wind rose in the afternoon and drifted the wrecks of ships far down the coast. Many Persians were drowned or killed as they tried to get ashore. Xerxes's great fleet was shattered, and he had to think what he had best do without it.

He decided to go back to Asia. It was not wise for the king to be away too long. He sent back the remains of his fleet to protect his bridge of boats. He divided his army, leaving many of his fighting men to winter in northern Greece. With the rest he went home, making the best of what he had done.

The Greeks were amazed by the result of their victory. Gladly the Athenians came back to rebuild their homes. Meanwhile, the captains of the fleet cast votes to award a prize of valor to the man who had done most for their victory.

Each man voted for himself, eager for honor for himself and his city. No first prize could be given. The second prize, by consent of everyone, went to Themistocles.

The Athenians had beaten the Persians by sea. It was now the turn of the Spartans to beat them on land. When the army which Xerxes had left behind came south in the following spring, it was met by the Greek army just north of Athens. Everyone fought bravely, but the great victory was mostly due to Spartan training. The bravest man on the Spartan side was Aristodemos, who died after doing wonderful deeds of valor. The Spartans talked him over and decided that he had wanted to die and prove to his people that he was not a coward. This was all very well, but others who had done brave things and died had wanted to live. The Spartans thought that these were better men and gave them the honor of a public funeral, refusing any reward for Aristodemos. The Spartans did not believe in forgiving mistakes.

VIII

Pericles, the Athenian
495–429 B.C.

AFTER its defeat on land, the Persian army left Greece, never to return. A little country had defeated the greatest empire that ever was seen. The Athenians thrilled with excitement. They wanted to free the islands of the Aegean and even the Greek cities of Asia Minor as well.

The Spartans wanted to go back home. They were not a sea people, and they never believed in fighting at a distance. They thought it bad for their simple citizens to travel and learn foreign manners.

The two cities went different ways. The Athenians became head of a great fleet to which other cities or islands gave ships or money. Soon nearly all of them preferred to pay money. The Athenians began to think that as long as they protected the rest, they might use these funds for themselves. The league against Persia had in twenty years become the Athenian Empire.

In the following years Athens became the wonder of the world. So many great men were born and lived in her, so many things were done which we still admire, that we call the days of the Athenian Empire a golden age. Many people have envied the Athenians, who thought nothing too great to do for their beautiful city.

It is time to take a look at this city of Athens and see what it was like at the moment of its glory. The first thing to notice about it is the way all Athenians shared in what went on. At the time of the Salamis battle, Athens had been a democracy for about thirty years. The Athenians did not mean exactly what we do by democracy. Indeed, in many ways they were more democratic than we are.

They did not elect men, as we do, to make laws. The Athenian Assembly was an assembly of all the citizens. When it was called on to meet, men cleared the market place by going through it with a rope dripping with red dye. If anyone hung back long enough to get a red mark on him, he paid a fine. In most cases, however, the Athenians wanted to take part. Their word for a man who did not care for politics was "idiot." It has changed its meaning somewhat since that day, but you can see that it was not a compliment.

The Assembly passed laws, but it was too big to carry on daily business. For this, the Athenians had a council of five hundred, but they did not elect it. They simply chose it by lot from all the citizens. It stayed in office a year and was divided into ten groups of fifty, each of which was on special duty for a tenth of the year. The president of the group of fifty which was in office was the president of Athens. He called the Assembly together and took the chair. He received envoys and did other important things. But every day a different man was president. The Athenians thought anyone, just picked by chance, ought to be good enough to be head of the state.

Was that true? And if so, why? How was it possible that the business even of a single city could be carried on in such a way? Besides, the Athenians were head of an empire and conducting a war. We cannot think that they were all clever men or military experts. If we want to see how the Athenians really managed their affairs, we cannot do better than follow the fortunes of the wise leader who gave his name to the golden age.

Pericles was born about 495 B.C., so that he was probably fifteen at the time of the battle of Salamis. The night before he was born, or so it is said, his mother dreamed that she had produced a lion. This pleased his father, for Greeks believed that dreams foretold the future. In any case, however, the birth of a boy was an important event. The baby was laid at the feet of his father, who had to receive him into the family by lifting him up. A wreath of olive was hung on the door to tell the neighbors that it was a boy. They used a white woolen ribbon if it was only a girl.

We need not follow Pericles through babyhood and school. He grew up a handsome young man, except that his head was oddly high and pointed. His father came from one of the richest families in Athens and was an important general. He died while Pericles was still a young man, but he may have been able to give his son experience. In any case, Pericles was related to people who had many ways of learning about public affairs.

The Athenians had no income tax, but they did have a rule that wealth ought to be spent in the service of the state. Rich people undertook unpaid jobs for their city. The state, for instance, paid for the food and crew of the warships; but the captains were rich men who paid for outfitting and repair out of their own pockets. Anyone too old to serve himself might put a relation like Pericles in command. It gave him experience, and his fellow citizens would learn to trust him.

Other things that rich men did were often connected with the festivals of the city. A man who has produced a few plays, arranged a procession, or trained a team of dancers for a competition becomes used to running things. A young man like Pericles, whose relatives are busy with such projects every year, finds plenty of chances to learn, even if his own turn does not come. If he wants to travel, he may be taken along by men who will be going at their own expense to represent Athens in some discussion with their neighbors. If, on the other hand, envoys come from abroad, he will get to meet them. Though Pericles had no more chance to be president of Athens than any country peasant, he was in a far better position to gain experience.

This training would have made Pericles a useful citizen, even in his early manhood, but it did not, by itself, make him important. He rose in politics by way of the law courts.

Athenian trials were exciting events, since the Athenians rather enjoyed going to law and loved argument. Athenian juries were very large: 201,

301, or even more jurors. When Pericles came into power he put through a law which gave the jurymen pay and made it possible for poor people to take the time from other business. Even before this law, a great many citizens heard legal arguments. Like all clever people when books are scarce, the Athenians loved speeches. Pericles proved to have a gift for argument and great dignity as a speaker. The first time we hear of him in public life, he is acting as prosecutor in an important political trial.

From speaking in the law courts to speaking in the Assembly was an easy step. If it had been possible for any man to jump up in the Assembly, nothing would ever have got done. Certain officials had the right to speak if they wished, and the president could call on important people. Pericles, with his rich friends, his wide experience, and his natural ability, soon gained a hearing.

Presently he went further yet and ran for office. There was one office which the Athenians did not dare choose by lot. Not everybody is fit to be a general. The Athenians elected ten generals every year, letting the Assembly decide between them when it came to a war. Just because they were elected, these ten generals were important men in Athens. Pericles was not really gifted as a general, and he was seldom put in charge of an army. The Athenians chose him as the statesman whose opinions counted for most in their Assembly. For nearly thirty years they went on electing him, so that this time is often called the Age of Pericles.

What was this age like? Let us hear what Pericles thought of it himself. Toward the end of his life he made a speech to the Athenians over those who had died in war. A great historian who heard Pericles speak many times has given us an idea of what he said.

First Pericles praises the freedom of his city, its liberal education, its love of beauty and wisdom. No other city, he points out, provides so many pleasures for the spirit in the shape of festivals, contests, and beautiful buildings. Yet when it comes to a fight, the Athenians are just as brave as the Spartans and have much more to fight for. "I claim," he says, "that our city as a whole is an education to Greece and that her members yield to none, man by man, for an independent spirit, many-sided abilities, and confidence in body and in mind."

For such a city it is good to die. It is also natural that those who survive should wish to spend their lives in her service. "That, indeed, is why I

have said so much about the city. I wished to show that we have more at stake than those who have no such inheritance." The men who died were not all heroes, but by their death they have made up for shortcomings. Pericles knows that for love of Athens they were glad to do so. "They were all alike," he concludes, "swept away from a world filled for their dying eyes not with terror, but with glory."

IX

Red and Black

480–430 B.C.

W H A T with fighting and governing and serving on big juries, Athenians were busy men. It
was easy for Pericles to give all his time to his
city, but other people had to earn their living.
They thought themselves lucky to be able to
have some of the hard work done by slaves.

Most Athenian households were small and did
not have many slaves. A country farmer who
brought his crops into Athens for sale might
have a servant who worked with him in the
fields. If he were well off, his wife would have a
girl to help with the children and the house-

work. A shoemaker or an armorer in town would have several workers. Unless he was a brutal, ill-tempered man, he treated them kindly; but he expected them to go on working while he took time off.

Many of these slaves were prisoners of war. Some Persians and perhaps even some of those poor Ethiopians and Indians drafted by King Xerxes may have ended up as slaves in Athenian households. Other captives were Greek, since the cities often made war on one another. Slaves were bought from Asia or Egypt, and even sometimes stolen as children.

The luckiest slaves in Athens were the skilled craftsmen. A shop was a place where things were made as well as sold. The shopkeeper was a craftsman working with two or three servants. A customer could either pick out what he liked or order something special. Let us take a look, for instance, at the workshop of one of the famous potters of Athens.

Streets in Athens were not named. They were narrow and winding and had grown up anyhow.

About 450 B.C., the Athenian port of the Piraeus, which was on the coast a few miles away from the center of the city, was laid out in blocks by an early town planner. In Athens itself it was difficult to find your way about. Luckily the potters, the sandalmakers, and the other tradesmen of the city all had their special streets, so that we should not have to hunt all over the city for the one shop we wanted.

The potters were important tradesmen. No Greek household could get along without a number of pots and jars. Water was carried and often stored in them. Oil, grain, and wine were kept in them too. Cups were needed, and bowls to mix wine with water. Tiny jars carried scented oils and toilet things. Many pots were simple, but the Greeks liked to make them beautiful as well.

If we followed a man who went in to buy a cup, we would probably find the potter sitting at his wheel and shaping a bowl on it. This takes a good deal of skill, as we can see today by visiting a craft shop. The Athenian potter learned his trade from his father and worked at it all his life. A rich customer who wanted a cup for special parties would go to one of the experts. We know of a famous one whose name was Euphronius. Behind him as he worked, some of the bowls he had just made would be standing on a shelf to dry and waiting for their stems and handles to be fitted on.

Euphronius would have a slave for the hard work like mixing the clay, getting water from the fountain down the street, or carrying wood for the furnace. Because the slave was unskilled, Euphronius would probably attend to the actual baking himself. The furnace was tricky. He had to use first dry wood, then green, then dry again, while he fiddled with dampers to control the smoke. If he did not get these exactly right, his paint would not turn into a rich black color which stood out against the red of the baked clay. Experts like Euphronius prided themselves on never making a mistake.

Customers might admire the graceful shape of several cups standing half dry on a shelf, but

they knew they could find something like them in other shops. Rich men would come to Euphronius for a cup decorated with one of the lovely pictures which made his shop famous. Euphronius, as it happened, painted himself; but as he grew older, some people thought him out of date. They preferred the younger artists in his workshop.

Two of these are men whose names we know. Panaetius, perhaps, might be seen drawing a design with a stick on the half-dried clay, while Onesimus used the paint. It would be hard to see what Onesimus was doing because the black color did not show until it had been baked. Onesimus worked on red-figure vases, painting in the background and leaving the figures of his design to stand out in red. This allowed him to draw clothes or faces with fine black lines.

We do not know whether these two painters were relatives or slaves of Euphronius. Their working tunics were just like Euphronius' own. He knew they were real artists, and so he would not interrupt Panaetius in the midst of his drawing or order Onesimus about. Unless he had a special order to fill, he would not tell them what to draw. Anyone who looked over his shelves of finished cups could tell that his men had a free hand. Some of the people in their paintings were gods or heroes. Other pictures showed boys at school, craftsmen in their workshop, or athletes cleaning themselves after practice. Every design fitted into the curves of the vessel on which it was drawn. Clearly Euphronius was as proud of his workmen's talents as he was of his own. Onesimus and Panaetius may well have been slaves; but if so, they were lucky ones. They were true craftsmen.

Slavery is never happy, even if some slaves are well treated. It is sad to know that some Athenian slaves were treated very cruelly indeed. The famous silver mines which brought wealth to the Athenians were worked by thousands of slaves. These crawled or lay in tunnels, two or three feet high and about the same width. They worked a ten-hour shift by the light of tiny oil lamps. They were naked, or nearly so, and they were chained to the rocks at which they hacked with short-handled picks. Many slaves died in these mines, and some Athenians who thought themselves good men made huge profits. The Athenians, we must remember, were at least no worse than our own century. Many people have been starved or cruelly treated in our times, and we have not yet been able to put an end to this. We can see, however, that slavery leads to this sort of cruelty. Even the Athenians, who prided themselves on being good to their slaves, never thought of the miners.

X

The Parthenon
447-432 B.C.

PERICLES taught the Athenians to use the
wealth of their empire for making their city
beautiful. Athenian houses were still simple, but
public buildings both in the market place and
on the Acropolis became the pride of all. King
Xerxes had done the Athenians a service by
burning their ancient buildings and clearing the
ground for better ones. Pericles and his archi-
tects designed a stairway on the Acropolis giving
access to new temples sacred to various gods, all
grouped around the Parthenon, the temple of
the goddess of Athens.

The Parthenon, 447–432 B. C.

The Parthenon is a very simple building. It is a long, barnlike structure built to contain Athene's image and a separate room behind to store her treasures. Around this runs a row of fluted columns, which are doubled at the front entrance and the back. Over all rises a gently sloping roof. The beauty of the Parthenon lies in its handsome shape, in its dignity, and in the care with which every detail has been thought out. Each column, for instance, is slightly thicker in the middle than it is at bottom and top. If you look at the building you cannot notice this, but it gives the columns a solid look, counteracting the effect of the light seen through them. In the same way, the platform on which the whole is set swells upward a very little in the middle of the long sides, thus looking firmer to the eye than if it were quite straight.

Decorations everywhere are perfectly plain, simply background for the sculpture which adorns the building. The name of the artist who designed these works was Phidias, one of the greatest sculptors of all time. He was about the same age as Pericles and an Athenian, but he had studied under a master in the Peloponnese. Greek sculpture was not by any means all Athenian, but at this moment it was starting an age of splendor of which Phidias is the greatest master. His style is deeply religious, simple and beautiful, standing midway between the stiffness of the past and the naturalism of the future. It fits the grandeur of the Parthenon.

Over the front entrance in the shallow triangle formed by the roof, Phidias set a group of figures representing the birth of Athene, the goddess of wisdom, who was said to have sprung from the head of Zeus. He could hardly show this actually happening, but he placed Zeus in the center, taller than the rest, with Athene beside him. Lesser gods sitting or lying in graceful groups fitted into the shape of the structure. In the extreme corners two horses' heads appeared. On one side the horse of the sun is shown rearing up to mount the heavens, while on the other side the horse of the moon is sinking wearily under the earth.

The remains of these sculptures, together with those from the other end, showing the contest of Athene and Poseidon for Athens, are not on the Parthenon today, but in London. If you ever go to the British Museum where they are, be sure to notice how the backs of the figures, which would never have been seen against the building, are as carefully finished as the fronts. Phidias and his fellow masons thought no trouble too great for the temple of Athene.

Another glory of the Parthenon was a frieze which went around the outside of the building, carved in a low relief. It showed the annual pro-

cession of the Athenians to offer their goddess a robe which had been specially woven by a group of maidens. If we walked around to the back or western entrance to the temple, we would see parts of the procession still forming up. Groups of young horsemen, gay in their best clothes and some in crested helmets, were tying their shoes or standing by their horses. Others had started already and went prancing down both long sides of the building, looking a little grave as they kept their mounts in position. In front of these went men in chariots who would compete in some of the races which were to follow later in the day. Before them came groups of men on foot, including other athletes. Ahead of these walked the animals for sacrifice, both cows and sheep, kept in position by their drovers. As the procession turned around the corners of the building to come together over the main entrance, we would see young girls with baskets of flowers or cakes and other things which were used in the worship of the goddess. Above the entrance, the gods sat on stools to watch, and in the center a priest and a boy unfolded Athene's garment.

This beautiful frieze, as well as the great groups of statues, was designed by Phidias, who must have made clay models which were copied in marble under his direction. It does not seem likely that he himself carved any, since he could hardly have had time during the fifteen years that the Parthenon was being built. His chief work was the great statue of Athene, over thirty feet high, made of gold and ivory. Unluckily for us, this famous statue was broken up for the sake of its gold some centuries later, but we have a few small models of it which show that Athene stood holding out a figure of victory on her right hand and resting her left on the round shield which was beside her. The folds of her golden dress were simple, but her breastplate, her shield, her helmet, the sides of the platform on which she stood, the very edges of her sandals, were decorated with figures. Her great round shield showed a combat scene into which Phidias had put himself, a bald man with an ax in his hand. Another figure bore the face of Pericles.

The Athenians, stunned though they were by the splendor of the image, were furious at Phidias. They thought it an insult to the goddess that a real man should appear on her armor. So angry were they that they tried him for what he had done and forced him into exile. He went to Olympia, where he was already famous for a great image for the temple of Zeus which was even more admired than his Athene. It too has vanished. All we have left in memory of Phidias is a little clay cup which says on the bottom that it once belonged to him. But the Parthenon statues which he designed have preserved his greatness forever.

The statue of Athene was melted down some centuries later, but for many hundreds of years the Parthenon stood almost unaltered. Unfortunately, in 1687 Athens was bombarded by the Venetians, who hit the Parthenon, which was being used by the Turks to store explosives. The center blew up and much of the sculpture was damaged. Nothing was done to repair it, but in 1801–3 the remains of the sculptures were rescued and taken to London. Not unnaturally, the present Greek government wants them back. The English reply that, had they been neglected for another century, much more would have disappeared. These priceless statues were given away by the rulers of the time and have at least been carefully preserved.

XI

The Great Dionysia

To The Athenians, the most important god after Athene was Dionysus or Bacchus, god of wine, in whose honor they held festivals of spring and harvest. From early times the Athenians had staged contests between groups of singers and dancers at the spring festival of Dionysus, which they called the Great Dionysia. A circular dancing place of trodden earth was built at the foot of the Acropolis, whose sloping sides formed a semicircle about it. In the center of this dancing place, which was called the orchestra, stood an altar to Dionysus.

We do not know how soon it was that the leader of the chorus began to stand out as a soloist who answered questions or recited stories about the gods and heroes of legend. After a while he began to act out what he said, dressing first as one character and then as another, and changing his costume in a small tent behind the orchestra while the chorus was singing. Just before the Persian wars, a very great poet who was writing at that time created drama by bringing onto the stage a second actor.

This poet's name was Aeschylus, and he is the first of three playwrights who made Athens famous for the better part of a century. A story says that Aeschylus as a middle-aged man fought in the battle of Salamis against the Persians. Sophocles, the next in age, was a beautiful boy of sixteen who was chosen to dance in one of the choruses to celebrate the victory. Euripides, the youngest, was born on the day of the battle.

Athenian tragic drama as invented by Aeschylus was very different from a modern play. It did not follow that, because he used only two actors, there could be only two characters. But only two speaking parts could appear on the stage at once, though silent attendants were allowed. What is more, since one actor played several parts, his separate characters could not come on together. Meanwhile, the chorus was present all the time, thus preventing the changes of scene that we are used to.

The use of only two actors was made easier because of a custom which seems strange to us. The actors of Greek drama played in masks. Each separate character had his own mask, so that it was perfectly easy to see at a glance which role the actor was playing. Probably the masks were convenient, too, because in the days before stage lighting it might not have been easy to see an actor's expression from the top rows of seats. Masks were carved and painted with great care to show the kind of character they belonged to; they also were highly colored and easy to see from a distance. Mouths were open so that the actor could be heard through them, and eyes were slitted or transparent so that he could see to move about. If we remember that Greek drama grew out of dancing and that it always had a chorus which was trained to dance and sing, we can compare it to modern ballet and understand better why people enjoyed it.

Perhaps you think that once Aeschylus had brought in the second actor, he might just as well have put in a few more. He might have used women for his female parts, stopped the actors playing in masks, or written some of his play in prose instead of verse. We have to remember that the Great Dionysia was sacred to the god, who might not have liked too many changes at once. Besides, Aeschylus did not need the freedom of our modern writers. Let us take a look at one of his plays in order to see what he could do.

Prometheus Bound opens with the god of fire and two demons with hideous masks, to express their brutal natures, chaining the enemy of Zeus to a rock. The fire god pities his prisoner and begs for a word of pardon, explaining that he only does what he is ordered to do. The leader of the two demons is brutal and coarse. The

other demon, who is merely an attendant, not an
actor, does not speak. The prisoner, whose si-
lence shows his unforgiving pride, is at this moment only a cardboard figure. When his captors
have done their worst and gone away, one actor
will slip around behind the rock and, placing
himself behind Prometheus, will call on heaven
and earth to witness the injustice of Zeus.

After this fine speech, the chorus enters, dancing to the music of a flute. It consists of sea
nymphs, daughters of Ocean, who have come out
of pity for Prometheus. He tells them how he
helped Zeus overthrow the old gods and bitterly
complains of his reward. Zeus thought little of

Man, whom the old gods had created; and he decided that Man must perish from the earth in order to leave room for new creatures. In pity Prometheus stole fire from heaven and taught Man the use of metals and the beginnings of civilized life, with the result that Man did not die. Zeus, thinking that force was the answer to all problems, has punished Prometheus savagely, but without effect. Prometheus cannot be killed because he is a god, and his pride is not broken.

The second actor now appears again as the god Ocean. He has on a new mask with a fine beard. Very likely he has built-up shoes under his long robe to make him look taller, and he may be padded out larger than life size as well. He does not need to move much, but he must be dignified. Ocean is one of the old gods but is still in power. The audience knows that Poseidon will soon thrust him aside; but for the moment Ocean thinks he knows how to manage Zeus with the loss of nothing but a little dignity. He comes to tell Prometheus he should give in to Zeus. But the savior of Man, who has done nothing but good, is too proud to say that he is sorry.

Ocean goes away, while the chorus sings the lament of the earth for the sufferings of its savior. Soon the second actor enters again in the mask and robe of a young girl. He needs not only to look different, but to speak differently. Athenian actors were judged mostly by their voices. Io, like Prometheus, is a victim of Zeus, who has first loved her and then left her to the jealousy of Hera, who drives her in torment over the world, never allowing her rest. The appearance of Io reminds us that Zeus is everywhere unjust, but it also hints at an end to the story. Prometheus knows that Io's descendant will one day release him, though he is not yet sure how this will come to pass. However, he has one power over Zeus. He knows a secret which Zeus must learn or he will be destroyed. What this is, he does not say; but his audience knows the legend and is aware that Zeus is starting with another love affair which is fated to be disastrous to him. Only Prometheus can warn him against it.

Once more the daughters of Ocean sing and

dance. The next to enter is Hermes, messenger of Zeus, with his staff with the twisted snakes and his winged sandals. Hermes, like his master Zeus, is angry. Zeus has heard the talk of the secret, and he will apply terrible tortures if Prometheus refuses to tell it. Again the victim defies his conqueror. The daughters of Ocean cluster about Prometheus, choosing to go with him to his place of torment under the earth. Then amid thunder and clashing rocks Prometheus utters his defiance once more as the play closes.

Prometheus Bound is the simplest of Aeschylus's great plays. For the whole of the action except for the opening, one of the actors is chained to a rock, while the other dresses up as people who come to speak to him. Yet out of this Aeschylus has created a lofty religious drama in which the savior of Man appeals to something higher than brute force. In a later play, which has been lost, Zeus must learn new values, while his great victim must put away pride. Thus behind *Prometheus Bound* we see the shadow of

Prometheus Unbound, which followed it. This may remind us that each poet wrote four plays for the Great Dionysia. Three were tragedies and often different parts of the same story. The fourth was a lesser piece, partly comic, of which no full examples have survived.

If a poet wanted to write for the Dionysia, he sent his four plays in good time to the Archon, who was one of the Athenian officials for the year. The Archon chose the three best dramatists, and gave each a chorus paid by the state. Three rich men were chosen to present the plays, which meant that they paid for the costumes, the masks, and the actors. By the middle of our period Sophocles, the second poet, had made two more changes. The first of these was a third actor, which meant that plays could be far more varied. The second was scenery painted on canvas, which was paid for by the patron.

Long ago the little tent in which the chorus leader used to change costumes had grown into a background to the stage. It had three entrance doors which were supposed to come from a nearby house, from the city, and from a far distance. But by painted canvas the artists could express a scene better and even sometimes change it. Certain devices had been invented to help the action, such as a high platform on which a god could appear in the air, or ropes by which he could be let down from heaven to earth. There was even a platform that could be wheeled out, on which events that had taken place indoors could be shown. In such a way did Clytemnestra appear, bloody weapon in hand, standing over the murdered body of her husband, King Agamemnon.

The Great Dionysia took five days. All the city and the outlying districts came in for the festival, which opened with a day of sacrifices, processions, and worship. At sunrise of the second day the theater was packed with people. By the time of Pericles the slope of the hill had been smoothed into a regular shape and filled with wooden benches, except for the front rows, where stone seats were kept for the priest of

Dionysus, the city officials, famous people such as Olympic victors, and the sons of men who had fallen in battle for their country. The whole theater held about seventy thousand; and any citizen, together with his household, might attend. Even women were allowed to go to the Great Dionysia. To avoid overcrowding, tickets, little tokens of lead, were sold in advance.

A few days beforehand the City Council picked out a number of men as possible judges. On the first day of the festival ten of these were chosen by lot. On the last day their votes were written down and put into an urn, which was taken to the Archon. He drew out five, and on the votes of these the prize was awarded. Thus the Athenians allowed the god to speak through the casting of lots, yet kept the right to choose sensible judges. When the winners were announced, the poet and his patron were crowned with ivy. In later days a prize was given to the best actor also.

If you had been present in the days of Pericles,

you would probably have wished Sophocles to win. Aeschylus was already old-fashioned, but Sophocles expressed in his own way the perfect beauty of the sculptures of Phidias. Besides, everybody loved him. Sophocles was not only good-looking, but witty and charming. He was not only a poet, but an able man who took part in public affairs. Even in his eighty-ninth year he could still write a fine play. Truly Sophocles was loved by the gods and might have been chosen by Solon as one of those he counted happy.

Eighteen times in his long life Sophocles was crowned with ivy. There were plenty of other poets, whose plays have all perished, and there was Euripides too. But Euripides was only crowned four times.

Euripides was too critical a poet to please those who knew him best. He was most famous outside Athens, especially among the young men. They liked the way he told the old legends as modern stories filled with modern people whose wickedness or folly brought on tragedy.

They even liked him to mock at the gods, showing bad actions which they were said to have done.

Euripides loved Athens, yet even during the golden age he saw her faults. Euripides was hardly fifty when a great war broke out between Athens and Sparta which many cities joined out of jealousy of Athens. War is a great breaker of ideals; and the Athenians, as the struggle went on, grew desperate. About sixteen years after the war had started, they demanded submission from a little neutral island called Melos, which was well placed for their purposes perhaps, but had not done them harm. The Melians, though they had no power to resist the Athenians, refused. Then the Athenians wished to make an example of Melos, and so they killed all the men, sold the women and children into slavery, and sent out colonists of their own.

This crime of the Athenians, which is hard to believe if the nature of the war is not understood, broke the hearts of many who remembered greater days. Next year at the Great Di-

onysia, Euripides produced *The Trojan Women,*
one of the best antiwar plays ever written, in
which the women of Troy, their men all dead,
are waiting to hear their fate. Not a word is said
about Melos, but the Athenians knew what he
meant. Bitterness grew between Euripides and
the city he truly loved, which increased as the
war went on. In the end he was driven into
exile and died in Macedonia, a country in the
north of Greece which was to be important for
the future. Sophocles, who was still living,
though a great age, led his chorus onto the stage
at the Great Dionysia, all dressed in mourning
for his fellow poet.

XII

Life and Death of Socrates

469–399 B.C.

I N T H E year 469 there was born in Athens a boy with the love of truth in his soul. Socrates was not of a great family like that of Pericles. His father was a stonemason, and Socrates himself may have worked on the Parthenon, perhaps dressing some of the big marble blocks or fluting the pillars. It seems unlikely that he was skillful enough to carve the statues which Phidias had designed, for he never worked hard at his trade. Socrates did not even look like a great Athenian, for he was an ugly man in a city where beauty was admired. His nose was broad, his lips were thick, and he was clumsy in build, getting stout as he grew older.

We have seen how a boy in Athens was taught Homer and music and athletics. In his teens he received two years of military training. After this he was thought to be grown up; but he soon found that there was a great deal still to learn. In the age of Pericles, Sophists, or wise men, came to Athens from all over the Greek world, ready to teach in return for a fee. What a young man starting in life most wanted to know was how to get ahead.

The most useful thing he could learn was the art of persuading other people, which was needed in politics, law, or business. Even nowadays we can hear a man say, "Because *this* is true *that* must follow," without ever seeing that it does not follow at all. The Sophists taught logic, which is the study of the rules of argument, showing what follows or does not follow, and why. It often happens, too, that we cannot explain ourselves, even when we are right. The Sophists taught grammar, which helps you to say what you mean. They taught how to group your thoughts together and make them interesting. They even taught voice production, because in those days few letters were written, and speeches took the place of our daily papers.

In this way the Sophists showed people how to think and talk, but they did not entirely forget what people ought to think and talk about. Because they were paid for their lectures, Sophists taught only what people wanted to know. All the same, Hippias, who was an Athenian Sophist about twelve years older than Socrates, gave lectures on mathematics, astronomy, grammar, poetry, music, the heroic age, and handicrafts, as well as making his own discoveries in geometry. It is not a bad list. Others taught the meaning of dreams, which was a popular subject because dreams were thought to be messages from the gods. No doubt these lectures on dreams would seem strange to us if we heard them, but they often discussed religion, which is always an interesting subject.

During the age of Pericles, many people were

thinking about religion. Older men, like Aeschylus, retold legends in ways which brought out great truths; but younger people, like Euripides, were discontented with Greek religion as a whole. It had grown up in an earlier world when gods were thought of as being like nature, strong and beautiful, but not always kind or good to men. By now many were beginning to despise the gods of the old legends because of evil deeds that they were said to have done. Men were seeking for a religion which reflected their own ideas about good and evil. In other words, they were looking for God, even if often in ways which were different from ours.

Naturally the Sophists shared these ideas, but they were afraid of being unpopular with the people who paid them. Most of them felt it safer to keep some opinions to themselves. Other men, however, who did not earn their living by teaching, were brave enough to discuss what they pleased. Such people called themselves not Sophists, or wise men, but philosophers, or lovers of wisdom.

It would be impossible to sum up all the thoughts of the early philosophers about truth. Some of them, for instance, were what we should call scientists and invented the earliest theories about atoms. Others worked out a great deal of what we know as geometry. Others again made discoveries about space or the nature of the world. All of them tried to understand the human soul, to find out what was good and what was bad in life, and to know what the world was really like.

We can well imagine that young Socrates was not much interested in chipping stone when there were such things to think about. He neglected his business to hang around in the market place where there were handsome colonnades for people to linger in, exchanging ideas. His wife used to get angry with him because he grew poor. But Socrates, as long as he was not actually starving, did not care.

The first thing that he found out was that the Sophists did not really know what it was best to teach. Indeed, they did not care as long as they earned their money. Socrates saw that before he could teach anything he had to clear away a lot of rubbish from people's minds, to show them that they did not really know all they thought they knew. In order to do so, he used a method which people ever since have called Socratic.

Socrates would start by getting someone or other to say something which was generally thought to be obvious. A man might remark, for instance, "Justice means doing good to your friends and ill to your enemies."

"Well, let us consider this," Socrates would say. "To start with, you will agree that *this* must be true. . . ." And he would say something very simple.

"Why, yes."

"Well then, if that is so, does not *this* follow? . . . " And he would make another easy statement.

"Yes, indeed."

"Well then, . . ."

By simple steps like this, in a short time Socrates would have so confused his opponent that he would have to admit that he did not understand "justice" or "good" or "friends" or "enemies," because he could not explain how reasoning that seemed obvious at the time was not correct. Very often he simply went purple in the face and walked away while all the listeners laughed at him. Socrates had made another enemy.

The method Socrates used is not too difficult for clever people to imitate. In the age of Socrates, a number of young men soon learned how to make older people look silly. Not all of them saw, however, that Socrates was not amusing himself. He wanted to clear the ground so that he could begin to build new ideas. Only a few who listened really cared what "justice" was, or what "good" was either.

The time of Socrates was a testing time for the Athenians. The great war between Athens and Sparta which broke out in the last years of Pericles went on for nearly thirty years. As it became slowly clear that Athens was losing, men grew desperate. Dreadful things were done on both sides, but nobody had ever expected better of the Spartans. The best of the Athenians were horrified at themselves, and they lost faith in their own people. Those who were older blamed the young men for forsaking religion. Those who were younger blamed the old and said the democracy of Pericles had proved a failure.

The great war ended in 404 B.C. Athens was defeated. Men had to start again without their empire, their private fortunes ruined and their ideals shattered. A dictatorship was set up in Athens which many hated. Those in power put

people whom they disliked to death without trial. Next there was civil war between the democrats and their enemies. In 399 B.C. democracy was restored, but there was much bitterness in Athens.

The position of Socrates at this time was very awkward. He had taken no part in affairs under the dictator, and at the risk of his life he had refused to obey when he was ordered to arrest a man under suspicion. All the same, it was the young men who had set up this rule. Critias, their leader, whose name was now hated by all, had been one of those clever people who had hung around Socrates and learned his method. Alcibiades, a nephew of Pericles whom the Athenians blamed chiefly for their loss of the great war, had been another. Many simple people thought that these new ideas had caused all their troubles. The result was that Socrates was brought to trial for corrupting the minds of Athenian young people.

An Athenian trial took place before a big jury of several hundred, which was supposed to represent the people. There was no judge, and there were no lawyers. The accused man had to plead his own case, though most people hired someone to write a speech. It was not the custom for a man simply to prove that he was innocent. He was supposed to appeal to the pity of the jurymen as well by dressing in his oldest clothes and bringing his wife and children weeping into court to plead for mercy.

The trial of Socrates made a great stir. Many were angry with him, but he had good friends anxious to help. Socrates would listen to none of these, and he would not pretend that he was not innocent. He forbade his family to come to court, and he made no appeal to the jury. Instead, he got up quite cheerfully to explain his life. The oracle of Apollo at Delphi had once called him the wisest man in Greece. Socrates had wondered how this could be, seeing that though he wondered about the nature of justice and truth and goodness, he did not understand them. At last, however, he saw that he was wiser than other people because he knew he did not know, while they thought they did. He spent his life looking for truth, and he questioned other people to find out if they understood more than he. It was not his fault if they never had reasons for thinking as they did. Nor was he to blame for young men who had turned out badly, seeing that he had always told them to put the good of their souls ahead of success.

The jury who listened to Socrates were in difficulty. There were many among them who did not want to condemn an old man of seventy who was well known to them all and loved by many. But they were angry at him because they did not think he was taking them seriously. Why did he not ask for mercy like everyone else? Where were his wife and children? The jury stood for the Athenian people, and they suspected that Socrates was trying to be rude. Their democracy had only just been restored after civil war. For the sake of their dignity, jurymen felt they ought to teach Socrates a lesson. They condemned him.

How, then, was he to be punished? The system was that the accuser now made a speech demanding a penalty, and then the defendant in his turn proposed one. The jury simply voted between these two. Socrates's accuser, who saw how angry the jury felt, thought he might be severe. He asked for death.

This put Socrates in a fairly good position, for many people who had voted against him knew well that he did not deserve to die. But Socrates would not admit he had done any wrong. Instead of a penalty, he suggested that he be given free meals at the town hall, together with Olympic victors and other people who had done service to the state. His horrified friends pulled him down and whispered to him; and he got up again to say that they were willing to pay a fine for him. For his own part, since he owned nothing to speak of, he could not pay.

We can well understand why the jury condemned Socrates to death. He had forced them to defend their dignity. But Socrates himself had a greater dignity when he told them after the sentence that Death had run after him and caught him, but that Wickedness, which was far

more to be feared, had caught his accusers. "I shall go away," he told them, "convicted by you and sentenced to death, and they go convicted by truth of felony and wrong."

"Perhaps these things had to be so," he added, "and I think they are well."

So many people were dismayed at the result of this trial that the Athenians on the whole would have been pleased if Socrates had escaped from prison. He was loosely guarded, and his friends made all arrangements. But Socrates said that in good times he had lived by the laws of the Athenians. He would not set a bad example by breaking those laws now.

Socrates was allowed to see his friends in prison, and he spent the last night of his life talking about the immortality of the soul. In the morning he bathed, said farewell to his wife and children, and went on quietly chatting until evening came. Just before sunset, the jailer came to say farewell and burst into tears. Then Crito, who was talking with Socrates, said hastily, "There is still time."

"I should only make myself absurd in my own eyes if I clung to life," Socrates said. He sent a boy to tell the executioner that he was ready for the cup of poison.

When it came, he drank it calmly and comforted his weeping friends as he waited for it to take effect. He lay quietly down as the drug made him drowsy and, in the presence of those who loved him, passed away. His work, however, did not die, since he left behind him a pupil far greater than he, whose writings have made the name of Socrates famous forever.

XIII

Plato, the Good Philosopher

429–347 B.C.

P L A T O was born about 429 B.C., which is the year of the death of Pericles, when the great war with Sparta was already three years old. He was thirty by the time that Socrates died; and he had seen the ruin of Athens, the loss of her ideals, the dark days of the dictator, and civil war. It was not an age in which Athens was an example for Greece any more. Phidias had perished long ago; Sophocles, longest-lived of her great poets, was now dead. In such an age, many Athenians were looking for a leader to bring back the good old days. To those who knew him well, Plato seemed the very man to do this.

He had every quality which people admired. He was strong and athletic. Indeed, we are told that Plato was not his name, but a school nickname which was given to him because of his broad shoulders and skill in wrestling. Like Pericles, he was born of a noble family which was used to leadership. He had money and leisure to finish his education by learning everything that the Sophists could teach him. He was brilliantly gifted, so much so that he himself hardly knew whether he ought to become a statesman such as Pericles had been or a great poet like Sophocles. Above all, he was good; and Plato's goodness had a charm which is often the gift of a man who is born to be a great teacher.

He knew what high hopes people had for him, and he felt that his powers should be used. But somehow or other the times were never just right. He had nothing in common with the loud-voiced men who were popular with the people while he was growing up, leaders who put their own interests first, Athens a long way second, and the rest of the Greek world nowhere. After the war, a group of wealthy men whom Plato knew well took over power. He might have joined them, but he did not trust them. The dictatorship which grew out of their rule proved worse than democracy. Nearly everyone rejoiced when democracy was restored, so that for a moment Athens seemed to make a fresh start. Almost at once, however, the people committed the terrible crime of killing Socrates.

Like many other young men with plenty of free time, Plato had left the Sophists to listen to Socrates. But unlike the clever young men who found Socrates so amusing, Plato loved him with his whole soul. The brilliance of Plato's own mind and his natural goodness fitted him to understand the older man. Socrates was sure that anybody who really knew what goodness was would be good. The trouble is that we none of us do know this, even when we think we do. What is worse, in daily life we hardly try to. The general tries to win a war. The politician tries to stay in power. Even the wise statesman who works for the good of his country does not see clearly what "good" is and seldom thinks of the good of all mankind. As for the rest of us, we do things because they are fun, or because we are angry, or for some other such reason. If we really knew what goodness was, we should do only what is good.

Taught by Socrates, Plato found that before he could think of being a statesman or a poet, he had to know more about truth. He had written a set of plays for the Great Dionysia; but after talking with Socrates about what a poet ought to understand, he tore them up. The murder of Socrates—for he felt it was nothing less —disgusted him with democracy. He now felt that it was wrong to trust government to such ignorant people. On the other hand, he had seen how bad a dictator can become. Plato was growing less eager to take part in politics, but more aware that new ideas about government were wanted.

He was not the only man to have these notions. It did not need a clever man to see that things had gone wrong. In the age of Pericles,

Athens had come close to uniting Greece. She had failed; and the long war which had followed when Greek fought against Greek for thirty years was the worst thing which could have happened. After Athens was defeated, men looked for leadership to Sparta. They admired the Spartans for their hard living, their simple ways, and their love of their state. But the Spartans were too stupid to think of others. They were even old-fashioned in war, so that before long they were defeated by the Thebans, who in their turn became the strongest people in Greece. They too, it was soon clear, had nothing to offer. Everybody saw that war between Greek and Greek was a great evil, and yet nobody knew how to stop it. Men looked for a leader, but they found none. No city was great enough to unite the rest, and no person could think of a government which would give everyone justice.

Plato turned away from politics for a time, and he began to write about Socrates. He wrote the speech of Socrates at his trial as far as he remembered it. Then he wrote talks which Socrates had, or might have had, with other people. Plato was trying to show the world what Socrates had been like, but to do so he put much of himself into these dialogues. His own imagination, his way of sketching characters, his love for Socrates, made them live. Soon Plato began to carry some of Socrates' ideas further, so that the words which he put into Socrates' mouth became his own words. He was not trying to deceive people, but writing a new kind of fiction. Without exactly telling a story, he made arguments interesting by putting them into the mouths of different people. As Plato worked out his answers to the problems of his time, it was important to him that others should read them.

It was no use, Plato had decided, letting men govern because they were a majority, or even because they were richer, cleverer, or nicer than the rest. Good people, who are the only ones really fit to govern, are people who understand everything. They know mathematics and science and history and all the other subjects people study, and they have found out from all these what the world is like and what our place is in it. In other words, they are true philosophers, lovers of wisdom. Real goodness can only be reached through hard study.

It was all very well for Plato to say that only philosophers could be really good, but this is no help to most of us, since it means that good people have to be clever. Plato, however, agreed that there is a kind of goodness which we get from following the wisdom of better men. If only we could have true philosophers to rule us, he thought, we would learn from them how to be good and happy.

Plato looked around at the Greeks of his own day, and he saw that philosophers were not ruling anywhere and that it did not look as though they would ever do so. He began to collect around him young men who were important in their own little states and try to teach them to be philosophers. Sooner or later, or so he hoped, one of them might come to govern and would set an example to the world. Thus Plato found his life work as a teacher.

One of his earliest pupils was a young man called Dion who was very important indeed because he was brother-in-law of the dictator—or, as the Greeks called it, the tyrant—of Syracuse, which was the chief city in Sicily. The Greek towns in Sicily had a great enemy in Carthage, just across the sea in North Africa. The people of Carthage were always trying to conquer Sicily, so that the Greeks in those parts tended to fall under dictators, trusting for protection to some general who had been successful in their wars. Dionysius, who had made himself tyrant of Syracuse at this time, was a strong man who had united many of the cities of the island under his rule.

It is far easier to convert one man than to convert a whole democracy; and Dion, who was young and hopeful, begged Plato to come to Syracuse himself. Dionysius was a tough soldier, not a philosopher; but he was a clever man who valued culture in other people. Indeed, he tried to write poetry himself. He was a tyrant who did not trust many, but he was on good

terms with his wife and loved her brother Dion. Who knew how far he might be willing to be guided by the good philosopher?

Plato agreed to come, but as soon as he arrived in Syracuse, he saw that he had made a mistake. Dionysius liked to surround himself with famous men; but he did it to increase his own fame, and he expected flattery from them. He had no intention of taking advice. Plato had been born a free man in a free city and had been looked up to all his life. He was great and he was good, but he was not meek. Dionysius and he had a fierce quarrel. Plato found it wiser to leave, but Di-

onysius wanted revenge. He ordered the captain of the ship in which Plato sailed to sell him as a slave in Aegina, which was a city that was not on good terms with the Athenians.

The captain did as he had been told, but by this time Plato was too well known and admired to suffer by such treatment. He was rescued at once by a wealthy friend, who bought him from his master and set him free. Plato offered to repay the money he had spent, but he would not take it. Then Plato spent the price of his ransom in the service of his ideal. He bought a small property just outside Athens on which there was a pleasant grove of trees sacred to an old hero called Academus. Here he built a school to teach young people how to become philosophers. Because of the hero of the grove, Plato's school was called the Academy. In its memory many schools in many countries have been named academies.

Plato was founding something greater than even he understood. The Academy lasted for over nine hundred years, and both the Greeks and the Romans owed a great deal to its learning. But for the present Plato pressed on with his purpose of training the rulers of the future.

Time went by, and the Academy was nearly twenty years old in 367 B.C., when Dionysius died. He left his tyranny to a son named after himself. The young Dionysius was already thirty, and he ought to have been able to rule. He was of weak character, however; and his father had distrusted him. He had never been allowed to know anything about public affairs or take any part in government. Mostly he had spent his time on his hobby, which happened to be carpentry. The result was that Dion, Plato's old pupil, became his adviser until he found his feet.

Dion wrote again to Plato at once. Here really was a chance! Dionysius was ignorant and young for his age. His character had hardly begun to form itself. He was flattered by the suggestion that the most famous man of his time would come to teach him. Perhaps he was not clever, but at least he was willing to learn. Much might be done.

Plato came, and young Dionysius listened to him. Unfortunately Plato could not teach how to be good without first teaching how to think. He began with mathematics, and as the court followed its ruler's example, everybody had to study geometry. It bored them all. Dionysius, though in love with Plato's charm, was not fond of math. Plenty of people were waiting for a chance to whisper to him that he need not study if he did not like to. Besides, he soon became jealous when Plato talked to Dion about things which he did not understand.

Once more the great attempt failed. This time the victim was Dion, who was driven into exile. Plato was kept for a long time almost as a prisoner because Dionysius was too vain to let him go. He did not want the world to say he was not able to study with Plato, yet he would not pay the least attention to him.

Plato escaped at last and went back to the Academy. Dionysius governed so badly that Dion came back from exile and drove him out. But Syracuse was not fit to be ruled by a philosopher. Dion was unable to control the city, and in the end he was murdered by a man he had trusted. Plato was in his seventies by then and near the end of his life. He had had great influence, not only on his pupils, but on all the best thinkers of Greece. But the problem which he had set himself to solve was no nearer solution. Before philosophers could rule, the common people must change their nature, too. What use would it be to have leaders if no one would follow?

XIV

The March of the
Ten Thousand

401 B.C.

T H I S is the story of an adventure. The man who
told us about it was an Athenian called Xenophon, just a year older than Plato. He was an
active young fellow, fond of riding, who had
served in the Athenian cavalry. He had also
listened to Socrates; and though he had not understood him well, he liked his love of virtue.
To Xenophon, virtue meant simple things like
duty and discipline. He thought the Spartans
had won the war because they were better at
these than the Athenians.

Like many others, Xenophon did not know

what to do when the war was ended. He might have wanted to run a farm, for instance; but the Athenian countryside had been burned over and most of the olive trees had been cut down. His family had lost money in the war, and he did not know how to regain his fortune. In 401 B.C., he was still thinking this over.

The Greeks and the Persians had long ago made peace with one another, since both were too busy with their own affairs to think of foreign wars. Through the Greek cities on the coast of Asia Minor, Greeks had many dealings with the Persian satraps, or governors of those parts. Greeks and Persians were getting to know one another. A chance now arose for men of the two nations to act together.

King Darius II of Persia was a weak king mainly governed by his wife, who happened to prefer her younger son Cyrus to her elder one Artaxerxes. There was something to be said for the queen's choice, since Cyrus was a gallant prince who attracted devoted followers. Naturally, however, her actions caused great trouble.

The first thing the queen did was to get her favorite son made satrap of Lydia, which was the richest part of Asia Minor. In doing so, however, she made an enemy. Tissaphernes, who had been satrap before, was a great noble and related to the king. As satraps were usually left in power for their lifetimes and often succeeded by their sons, Tissaphernes was angry when he was left only a tiny part of Asia Minor. Since, however, he was a clever man, he pretended to have become an admirer of young Cyrus.

In 405 King Darius lay dying, and he sent for his sons. His disease was a slow one, which was lucky for Cyrus, as his satrapy was several months' journey from the Persian capital of Susa. All the same, it was bad news for him because his power was not yet as great as he hoped it would become. He knew that when the king died he would need his friends beside him, and so when he answered his father's call he took Tissaphernes with him.

A false friend is worse than no friend at all. Tissaphernes not only helped Artaxerxes to seize the throne, but also told him that Cyrus was in a plot to murder him. The young prince was thrown into prison at once, but luckily for him Artaxerxes was afraid of his mother. She was able to gain the release of Cyrus, who was sent back to his satrapy until his brother should dare to punish him.

Cyrus was too high-spirited to wait calmly for his fate. He began gathering an army at once under pretext of putting down troubles in Asia Minor. Cyrus liked Greeks, and he knew that Greek infantry was better than Persian. Besides, since the great war with Athens had come to an end there were many idle soldiers in Greece. Cyrus promised service under a Spartan general, who happened to be visiting him, as well as good pay and the chance of plunder. One of his friends persuaded Xenophon to come along, not as a soldier, but as a gentleman-adventurer. This gave Xenophon a better social position. If Cyrus ever ruled over the Persian Empire, who knew to what heights he might raise his friends? Expectations were in the air. Adventure beckoned.

Cyrus set out eastward from his capital city of Sardis in March of 401, as soon as the grass was green enough for his horses to forage. He had with him about ten thousand Greeks under the command of his Spartan friend Clearchus. He had also slingers and bowmen, Asiatic infantry, and twenty-six hundred cavalry, in which the Persians were always strong. All in all, including troops which he might pick up on the way, he would face his brother with nearly thirty thousand men.

The army of Cyrus started in good spirits. Most of the Greeks were tough characters, many homeless as a result of their wars. They had brought women with them to cook and help make camp, so that a vast train of carts and baggage was strung out along the royal road, which ran eastward all the way from Sardis to the king's palace at Susa in Persia.

Cyrus was still pretending that his purpose was to fight a small war in Asia Minor. It was not until they had marched through Asia Minor to the borders of Syria that his Greek forces became alarmed. They were by this time a long way from their homeland and at the eastern end of the Mediterranean. While they were still beside the sea, they felt sure they could get back home. What would happen to them, however, if Cyrus plunged into the wilds of Asia? They staged a mutiny; but Clearchus calmed them down and Cyrus promised extra pay. He said they were only going to fight against the satrap of Syria. He may indeed have thought he would have to do so, as he needed to go through a great pass called the Syrian Gates, where an army might have stopped him. But the satrap of Syria was waiting to see who would win. Cyrus passed through the Syrian Gates and turned eastward to Thapsacus, which lay on the river Euphrates.

Here at last he could pretend no longer. The Greeks were now very uneasy, but it was too dangerous to turn back. Behind them, the Syrian satrap had probably blocked the Syrian Gates. Cyrus promised fabulous things if he won, and it seemed likely that he would. Many, too, were encouraged because the Euphrates was unusually low. The army was able to wade across, even though the Syrian satrap had burned all the boats. They decided that the god of the great river was on their side as they bore southward down its eastern bank toward Babylonia.

The country in those parts was mostly desert; but they had supplies on their carts, and the river gave water. They saw ostriches in the distance. Gazelles could be hunted on horseback, and so could the game birds called bustards,

which did not fly well. Xenophon, who was well mounted, even joined a group to hunt the swift wild asses, whose flesh, he thought, tasted like venison when cooked on their camp-fires. The bulk of the army plodded on through the dust, their heavy armor on the carts. It was September before they reached Babylonia, and they had been marching for six months.

King Artaxerxes was lazy, and besides he did not yet know whom he could trust. The army he had gathered was only about the size of Cyrus' own and did not represent the real strength of his empire. It faced Cyrus at a little village called Cunaxa, just north of Babylon, which was too great a city to let go without a struggle.

Both brothers took their place in the center, where Artaxerxes put Tissaphernes with the best of his cavalry. Cyrus, whose cavalry was less strong, faced him with a mixed force. He had put Clearchus and the ten thousand Greeks on his right, while the rest of his infantry was on the left, each facing the infantry forces of his enemy.

As the battle opened, Clearchus charged with his men and easily scattered the troops opposite. He did not, however, turn to take Artaxerxes in the rear, perhaps because his hired soldiers were looking for plunder and for prisoners to hold for ransom. At all events they ran after their enemies without thinking about the rest of the battle. They opened a gap between themselves and the center into which Tissaphernes charged like a thunderbolt.

The battle was lost and won by that movement. Cyrus with six hundred horsemen made a desperate charge to save the situation, but his force was not strong enough. Fighting like a madman, Cyrus cut his way through his brother's bodyguard and even wounded the king. He was forced backward by superior forces and killed. With his death, there was nothing left for his army to fight for. The Greeks, returning in triumph, found themselves alone on the battlefield, surrounded by the king's victorious army.

Both sides encamped to think things over. The Greeks were six months from their base in a hostile land. Their camp had been plundered while they were pursuing their foes, so that they got no dinner. Battle had been joined before most of them had eaten breakfast.

They wanted to go home, but they did not have supplies for the route through the desert along which they had come. Luckily for them, Artaxerxes was only anxious to get them out of his kingdom. If they would agree to buy their supplies peacefully, he would leave Tissaphernes with an army to guide them homeward.

The Greeks piled their tents on the carts and set out bravely to march home. Tissaphernes led them south and eastward over the Tigris, where he turned north toward the Armenian mountains and the Black Sea, a very great distance away over unknown country. He was afraid that the Greeks would seize some strong place from which they could not easily be driven out. Clearchus held a meeting with him to persuade him that they really meant to go home. Tissaphernes invited the chief officers to dinner to show his better understanding. They went, not only Clearchus, but the lesser generals and the company commanders. Tissaphernes seized them all and sent them to Susa, where they were put to death by Artaxerxes.

For a short while the leaderless army panicked. But Xenophon and a few others who kept their heads told them that their lives depended now on their common sense. They chose new leaders, burned all their carts and tents so that they could move faster, and formed in a hollow square with pack horses and women in the middle. Tissaphernes, now openly hostile, followed close behind them, attacking them with cavalry and slingers. Xenophon, who had been put in charge of the rear, put together a mounted group to drive them off.

They went north along the bank of the Tigris, unable to cross it because it was swift and easily blocked by local forces. Tissaphernes hung on their heels till Kurdistan, where the country was so rugged that the hill tribes had never been conquered by the Persians. Here he left them alone; but they fared badly, struggling through endless passes where the natives rolled down great boulders on them from the cliffs.

It was a relief to reach Armenia, though this was Persian again and the local satrap was waiting for them with another army. Practiced marchers that they now were, they slipped around him, hurried through his satrapy, and got into Western Armenia. Here they found another satrap who was willing to let them cross if they would keep the peace.

It was winter in these parts, and snow fell heavily, and so they lodged their troops in several villages instead of all together. But before long they saw the campfires of a great army following them, and they no longer dared to separate. They had to camp on the open ground with nothing but their cloaks to protect them from a heavy fall of snow. Luckily there was plenty of food in the places round about, as well as pork fat and oil, which they smeared over their bodies for extra protection from the cold.

A prisoner warned that the satrap was setting an ambush, so that if they were to get away at all,

they must do so with speed. They crossed the Euphrates, high up and near its source, wetting themselves to the waist in its cold water. They meant to make for Gymnias across the mountains. This was a place they had heard of on the route to Trebizond, which lay on the shores of the Black Sea and was Greek. They soon found, however, that the snow lay too deep in the hills. They were forced to turn eastward along the banks of the Euphrates, marching for two days with a bitter east wind in their faces.

On the third day the wind became a gale and snow fell heavily. They camped in the open once more, lighting great fires. Most of them were

wearing rawhide sandals, hastily made to replace their worn-out shoes. These froze on their feet if they were not taken off at the stopping place, while the shrunken straps sank deep into swollen flesh. Men were suffering from frostbite and snow blindness. Some died of cold. On the next day, Xenophon, coming up with the rear guard, could not get the men to move, even though he told them that the enemy was at their heels. Luckily when he turned at bay, he frightened the pursuers off.

They found refuge at last in some underground villages where men and animals huddled together in burrows, smelly but warm. Here they were given a liquor made of barley which these wine drinkers thought extremely strong. It was, however, Xenophon found, very good indeed, once you got used to it.

These people were friendly, and the headman had offered to guide them; but the riffraff of the Greek force were by now out of hand. They carried off the chief's son, while Xenophon made matters worse by seizing for the rear guard seventeen fine horses being raised for King Artaxerxes. In revenge the headman led them far astray, and they wandered for a week. At last they plunged north again, fought their way through rough country, and came down onto a river valley which led them in eight days' march to Gymnias.

At Gymnias their troubles ought to have been over, but their guides misled them again. Five days later they found themselves climbing another mountain, and Xenophon heard shouting up ahead. He was used to trouble by now and merely thought that another wild tribe was holding them up. In their usual fashion they had burned the district behind them and had angry people on their heels. Xenophon took the cavalry and began to push past the baggage train to see what he could do. By now, however, the soldiers in front were passing the word back, so that it was running down the column. Everybody was shouting at the top of his lungs, and in a moment Xenophon could hear what they were saying.

"The sea! The sea!" they yelled. From the top

of the mountain they had caught sight of it at last. They were safely home.

Everybody broke into a run. Even the pack animals were prodded into a trot. Those who got to the top and saw the view threw their arms around one another, captains and generals as well, with tears in their eyes. Men started to pick up rocks and build a great heap to mark the spot of their deliverance. They even piled on their walking sticks, together with rawhide and booty from their latest fight. Then with light hearts they turned their backs on the land and went down to the sea.

We need not think that the Greeks of Trebizond were altogether pleased when a ragged army of ruffians, now no longer ten thousand, poured down from the hills into their city. Trebizond had not enough ships to send them home by sea and not enough food to support them for long. The town did its best and was lucky enough to see the Ten Thousand march westward before they got more out of hand. From there, their route, partly by land and partly by sea, led down the coast to the strait between Asia and Europe. They left behind them a trail of burned villages and angry townsmen, both native and Greek.

Despite their behavior, the men kept the rough discipline which had carried them across the Persian Empire. Indeed, their splendid march had given them a swagger. But when they saw the north Aegean at last, few had the money to pay their passage home. Fear and resentment made every city hostile. Xenophon was afraid for the fate of his comrades, and he stayed with them to keep them together.

Luckily for them, the Spartans, who had drifted into war with Tissaphernes, soon proved happy to hire the Ten Thousand to fight in Asia Minor. In this way Xenophon made his fortune at last by capturing a wealthy Persian and seizing his goods. He went on afterwards to serve in other wars, but the remains of the Ten Thousand who had made the famous march were scattered through Greece and passed out of history.

XV

Philip, the Strong King

359–336 B.C.

W E   C A N easily imagine how, after the march of the Ten Thousand, all Greece was full of old soldiers telling tall stories about their adventures and describing the vast wealth of Persia. They gave the impression that the Persian Empire had gone soft and that it only needed courage to cut one's way to its heart.

The adventure had a different effect on Xenophon. He had admired Cyrus and the Persian noblemen who were with him. They were hardy men and good fighters, fiercely loyal to their lord. At one time during the march the baggage wagons stuck in a muddy place, and Cyrus thought the soldiers were taking too long to pull them out. He ordered the nobles who were with him to show the men what they could do.

"They each threw off their purple cloaks," Xenophon tells us, "where they chanced to be standing and rushed, as a man would to win a victory, down a very steep hill, wearing their costly tunics and colored trousers, some of them with necklaces around their necks and bracelets on their arms. Leaping at once with all this finery into the mud, they lifted the wagons high and dry and brought them out more quickly than one would have thought possible."

Xenophon thought well of such men and of their prince, who had been trained from earliest boyhood to show himself brave, ready to honor other brave men, eager to be generous, but fierce against his enemies. Such people had a great deal to teach the Greeks, Xenophon decided.

Remembering what he knew of Cyrus and his Persians, Xenophon wrote a long essay called *The Education of Cyrus*. It was not about the upbringing of the Cyrus he had met, but about his ancestor, the great Cyrus, who had been founder of the Persian Empire. Xenophon, in fact, was thinking over the same problem as Plato. While Plato was trying to make the tyrant of Syracuse into a model ruler, Xenophon was describing the best training for a great prince. Instead of being taught math and philosophy, however, Cyrus learned riding, simple habits, honesty, loyalty, and courage.

When two such different men as Xenophon and Plato each imagine a great ruler as an example to Greece, it may well be that others are thinking of the same thing. Even possibly history may be going in that direction. The year before Plato started out to teach young Dionysius, something happened in the north of Greece which may not have seemed important then. King Alexander of Macedon was murdered by one of his nobles, who set himself up as regent in the name of the king's next brother, Perdiccas.

At this time, the Thebans were the strongest power in Greece; and they, being north of

Athens, were concerned about countries farther north still. Macedonia was not a city-state, but a kingdom, rugged and half savage. Except near the coast, most of its people were not Greek. When an earlier King Alexander had entered in the Olympic games at the time of the Persian wars, it had been objected that the games were only for Greeks. Alexander had satisfied the judges by claiming descent from Greek heroes said by Homer to have reigned in those parts. After that, it was agreed that the kings of Macedon, whatever their subjects might be, counted as Greek.

As time went by, the Macedonian kings became more cultured. They were an able family; and as they increased their control over their own tribes, they began to meddle with their neighbors. The murdered King Alexander had been laying claims to Thessaly, which lies between Macedonia and Thebes. Thus, taking advantage of the troubles which followed his death, the Thebans were glad to force a treaty on the regent. As the price of their support, he with-

drew from Thessaly and gave hostages for good behavior. Among these was the youngest brother of Perdiccas and Alexander, a lad named Philip. In this way Philip gained a Greek education, and a chance to study under two Theban generals who were the greatest military leaders of their times.

Philip spent three years in Thebes and returned to Macedonia to start taming the wild tribesmen and forming an army drilled in the tactics of the great Thebans. In 359, when Philip was twenty-three years old, Perdiccas died. He left an infant son, but since three half-brothers of the king as well as a couple of other pretenders were hotly claiming the throne, the Macedonians saw they needed a strong leader. They rallied around Philip.

Philip was exactly the man to appeal to a half-savage people. He was handsome, athletic, and daring, a fine rider, and always in the forefront of the battle. He could rough it with his soldiers and was not too proud to roar at their crude jokes. On the other hand, he was a great worker and organizer, determined to master his unruly subjects. His Greek culture helped him to deal with the cities to the south, or even those founded by the Athenians along the very coast of Macedonia.

In the first few years that Philip ruled in Macedonia, he was busy forming a national army. Soon he seized Amphipolis, an Athenian stronghold which gave control over gold mines just outside it. Under his rule, Macedonia grew rich, so that Philip's coinage became almost as well known in the Greek world as the silver "owls" of Athens.

Presently Philip attacked other towns which the Athenians controlled along his coast line. He took Potidaea; and on the day he did so, messengers came to him with good news. His horses had won the chariot race at Olympia, his general had defeated tribes in the northwest, and his queen had borne him a son named Alexander. Wise men assured him that the child born at such a lucky moment would become a great king.

By this time the affairs of the Greeks were once more in confusion. The Phocians had seized the temple of Apollo at Delphi and were defending themselves there by hiring armies out of the sacred treasures of the god. This outrage had plunged all Greece into war, and it gave Philip a chance to interfere. Pouring his army southward through Thessaly, he announced that he had come to restore the temple to Apollo.

This was all very well, but nobody imagined that when Philip had conquered Greece as far as Delphi he was going to go quietly home. The Athenians, who had been too busy with the troubles of Greece to interfere earlier, now roused themselves to block him by seizing the pass of Thermopylae, where once three hundred Spartans and their allies had held the Persian army.

This crisis of 352 brought to the fore in Athens a man who was to make himself the champion of Greek freedom. Demosthenes, born of well-to-do parents, had been left fatherless at the age of seven. He inherited a sword factory in which a number of slaves were employed, together with a large sum of money. This fortune, however, was so badly handled by his guardians that he found himself almost penniless when he grew up.

Demosthenes was furious, and he wished to take his guardians to court. This meant he would have to plead his own case, and he started to study the art of public speaking. How soon this led him to hope to rise in politics, we cannot tell. Before he could succeed at all, he had a good deal to overcome. He was thin and weedy with a narrow chest, a weak voice, and a slight lisp.

Anyone less likely to speak well in an open-air assembly could not be imagined. But Demosthenes, like Philip, was a hard worker.

We are told he taught himself to speak clearly by practicing with pebbles in his mouth. He trained his voice by reciting poetry against the sound of the waves on the seashore. He controlled his breathing by making speeches as he ran uphill. Because he had a nervous jerk of one shoulder, he hung a weight over it while he was practicing so that he bruised it every time he made the gesture. In the end, he learned to write fine speeches and to deliver them fairly well. He won back a part of his fortune, and he gained the ear of the Athenian assembly.

Demosthenes was an Athenian democrat who loved the cause of freedom as he saw it. Philip might be called Greek; he might even be a splendid ruler over a half-savage country. He must not, however, reign over the Athenians, who had done so much with their freedom. Demosthenes preferred the quarrels of the Greeks and their independence.

Meanwhile, Philip was a threat to the cities on the coast of Macedonia. He had built a fleet and was interfering with the grain trade from the Black Sea on which the existence of Athens depended. Demosthenes delivered the first of several great speeches against Philip which have been famous ever since as the *Philippics*. He wanted the Athenians to face their danger and go out to fight Philip themselves instead of hiring soldiers.

Philip was quick where his enemies were slow. He was clever enough to keep the Athenians busy by stirring up trouble for them at home. While they were busy with this, he took their chief stronghold in the north, sold its inhabitants into slavery, and wiped out thirty-two Athenian towns. As refugees trickled southward, Philip was celebrating his conquest by games and feasting in Macedonia.

Even Demosthenes was forced to admit that it was hopeless to fight Philip without the help of cities on the spot. Philip himself, who admired Athens, was eager to make peace. Demosthenes agreed to be one of an embassy to talk things over. In this way he had his first sight of King Philip, who was at this time a man of thirty-six, much scarred in battle, in which he had lost an eye, but vigorous as ever.

While Philip grew in power, another king had died. Artaxerxes II of Persia had proved a weak ruler under whom the empire had fallen into decay. His successor, Artaxerxes III, was more active, so that people who had been taking advantage of the state of affairs were better restrained.

None were more annoyed at this than the Greeks. From their positions on all the best harbors of Asia Minor, they had got the trade of the whole area into their hands. As secretaries and paid officials, Greeks were running the satrap's affairs. As hired soldiers, they were keeping up his power. It did not please them to have a king who wanted to control them.

Out of discontent with Persia, out of the stories brought back by the Ten Thousand, a feeling was growing. Greeks ought to rule Asia

Minor, perhaps the whole Persian empire. A national war against Persia would unite Greeks as it had done in the great days when Athens and Sparta had led them against King Xerxes.

Who was to lead them now? Who had the power but Philip? Isocrates, a famous statesman of Athens who was now ninety years old, wrote Philip a letter asking him to do so. The soldiers who fought for hire in every Greek quarrel were the real curse of the age. It was they who kept quarrels alive, who formed armies which burned and destroyed everywhere. Only Philip could drain them out of Greece and, having conquered Persia, could settle them in the East to act as outposts of empire and to spread the Greek way of life.

There was much truth in this, but Philip could see that the Greek states would not follow his lead unless he was their master. In 338 another quarrel arose over Delphi, and Philip was invited to interfere. This time the Thebans were on his side, and nothing could stop him. Marching rapidly past Thermopylae, he soon found himself only about forty miles from Thebes and seventy-five north of Athens.

The Athenians were alarmed and sent Demosthenes to persuade the Thebans to enter an alliance. Philip sent envoys, too; but they were no match for the fiery speeches of his chief enemy. Thebes and Athens swore friendship and started to gather their armies against Philip.

The two sides met on the plain of Chaeronea on the second of August, 338. The Thebans were on the right hand, faced by Philip's finest troops under the command of his son Alexander. Philip himself, by now so scarred by his battles that he was lame and had an arm disabled as well as being one-eyed, commanded against the Athenians on the left, who were in a good position on high ground. Alexander, charging at the head of his picked forces, outfought the Thebans. Philip made his men retire before the Athenians, who rashly pursued them onto level ground, thus throwing away their advantage. Presently the victorious Macedonians were able to turn on the center, which was defended by various smaller states and hired soldiers. A thousand Athenians lay dead on the field. Two thousand were captured. The rest of their army, which included Demosthenes himself, escaped over the hills in disorder.

The victory of Chaeronea made Philip master of Greece. He knew it and, rejoicing in his barbaric way, danced a drunken victory dance that very evening amid the corpses of the slain. The Athenian captives herded near the spot watched his antics in disgust, and Demades risked his life by calling out to ask if the great conqueror were not ashamed to act the drunken buffoon. But Philip, though half barbarian, was Greek too. He walked back to his tent, had the wine removed, and sent for Demades to give him his freedom.

Next morning it was as wise king and not as buffoon that he decided what he was going to do. On the Thebans, who had turned against him, he had little mercy. But the Athenians, who were putting their city in shape for a siege and had drafted men up to sixty years of age to man the

walls, were still the people whom he admired most in Greece. Philip was willing to be friends if the Athenians would become his allies and, in effect, his subjects.

The Athenians agreed because they had little choice. Philip was able to enter and gaze on the marvels of the Parthenon or visit the Academy of Plato. He was gracious, but the Athenians hated to lose their liberty. As a sign of their feelings they chose Demosthenes to deliver the speech over their dead in the battle.

Philip put garrisons at strong points in northern Greece and marched for the Peloponnese. No one made any move against him until he reached the borders of the Spartans. They, fewer in number than they had been, had not for some time been powerful in Greece. However, they still had their pride. Refusing to recognize Philip as their master, they sent him a blunt message in the old Spartan style.

"If you imagine that your victory has made you greater than you were, measure your shadow."

Philip wanted their good will and merely asked them if he might enter their country as a guest. When they refused this, he started to threaten.

"At any rate," the Spartans answered, "you cannot prevent us from dying for our fatherland."

"If I conquer your country," replied Philip in a rage, "I shall show you no mercy."

The Spartans sent him back a final message. It was, "If."

There was nothing to be done with these Spartans but deprive them of all power and leave them alone. Philip was busy forming a league of states to force internal peace and military union upon them.

Now Philip announced a great campaign against Persia. The time was ripe, for it so happened that Artaxerxes III had just been murdered, and the empire was in confusion. Troops were raised from all the states; and while things were getting ready, Philip celebrated the marriage of his daughter to one of his neighbors who was king of Epirus.

This wedding was a splendid occasion. Philip was at the height of his triumph, and his image was borne through the streets with those of the gods. He himself chose to walk alone in the wedding procession, telling his guards to lag a little behind so that he might be familiar with his people. Thus unprotected, he was struck down by one of his nobles who had a grudge against him. So perished the strongest man that Greece had ever seen. He was forty-six and had thought himself only at the beginning of his glory.

XVI

Alexander
the Great King

356–323 B.C.

ALEXANDER was twenty years old when his
father was murdered, the only son of the queen
Olympias, who had long ago quarreled with
Philip over his custom of taking extra wives like
the king of Persia. Partly for this reason, and
partly because Philip was busy with his wars, the
boy's education was left to his mother, who chose
for him a stern tutor. Leonidas would allow no
softness in the boy. He used to look through the
chest where Alexander kept his clothes and
blankets to be sure that the queen had not pro-
vided anything costly. He only allowed the plain-
est food, and he taught the prince that the best

"cook" for a good breakfast was an all-night walk, and for a good dinner was a light breakfast. In fact, he gave Alexander the sort of training which Xenophon praised in *The Education of Cyrus.*

When Alexander was about twelve, legend says, an incident attracted Philip's attention. A dealer had a great black horse for sale, which he called Bucephalus, or Bull's-head, because of the shape of a white mark on his forehead. He was indeed a splendid creature, but he would let nobody mount him. Philip told the owner to take him away, but Alexander said it was a shame to lose such an animal because nobody had the skill to ride him.

Philip was angry at his impudence, but the boy offered to bet the price of the horse that he could ride it. He had noticed that Bucephalus was frightened by his own shadow dancing on the ground in front of him. He turned him to face the sun and patted him until he quieted down. Suddenly he sprang on his back, and the horse bolted madly. Philip, who had never thought the boy would mount, was afraid for him now. Alexander, however, clung on until Bucephalus was tired enough to be guided safely home.

We shall never know if the story of how Alexander won his horse is a true one, but it gives a good picture of his cleverness and daring. Philip began to take interest in the boy, and shortly afterward he arranged another tutor for him who was in his own way the most famous man in the Greek world.

Aristotle had come to Plato's Academy when he was seventeen and had proved himself the best pupil Plato had. He had stayed there another seventeen years, learning and teaching, until Plato died. At this point he left the Academy to form a school of his own. Aristotle was a different kind of man from Plato. He did not have as much imagination, but he was more practical. When Plato, for instance, wanted to know what the ideal government might be, he started to consider what the soul of a man was like. When Aristotle asked himself the same question, he collected a hundred and fifty-eight different constitutions which had been set up by the Greek states; and he tried to compare them.

Now Aristotle, as it chanced, had been born in one of the Greek towns on the Macedonian coast. His father had been a doctor and was actually court physician to King Amyntas of Macedonia, Philip's father. Philip and he were about the same age, and shared childhood memories. Since then, Aristotle had learned in the Academy that Plato's purpose was to train the rulers of the future. For both these reasons, Aristotle was willing to tutor Alexander. Thus on top of the education described by Xenophon, Alexander received some of the training of Plato.

He never became a philosopher, but he was clever and eager to learn. Aristotle's position as tutor gave a special interest to the young heir of Macedon, as many remembered Plato saying that the ruler of the future must have this sort of education. Statesmen like Demosthenes who visited the court of King Philip thought it worth while to meet the boy.

They were nearly all impressed. Alexander

was striking-looking, with blue eyes and golden curls. He was tall for his age, and good at every sport. He loved poetry and music; and he liked to compare himself with his legendary ancestor Achilles, hero of *The Iliad,* who won great glory from his earliest years.

Philip soon gave his son military training. When Alexander commanded a wing in the battle of Chaeronea, he was only eighteen years old; but he had been fighting since he was sixteen, and he had also governed Macedonia while his father was absent.

When Philip died, his son was only twenty. Demosthenes urged the Athenians to regain their freedom. But his plans were upset by the energy of Alexander. The Athenians were forced to receive him as their master. They did not like him. Philip at least, many felt, had been a great man. The Athenians, who were unused to kings, sneered at this untried boy who wanted to be treated like a hero. When Alexander went on to Corinth, everyone laughed at what happened to him there.

There was a philosopher in Corinth called
Diogenes who felt that nothing mattered except
a man's own soul. To show his contempt for the
world, he dressed in rags, was unshaven and
dirty, and had no home but a big tub laid on its
side in which he took shelter when the weather
forced him to do so. He lost no chance of telling
the Corinthians what he thought of them for
caring about useless things, and he had become
famous for his rude remarks.

Curious, Alexander went to see him. They made a strange contrast as the golden-haired young man in the royal costume stood looking down at the rough philosopher who was squat ting in front of his tub. Diogenes took no notice of the king until Alexander asked if he could do anything for him.

There probably was no one in Corinth who would not have been glad to ask a favor of the master of all Greece. Diogenes looked up frowning at the tall young man in front of him and said, "Yes. Stop standing between me and the sun."

The Greeks laughed, but Alexander was not angry. He admired the philosopher's spirit and said to his friends, "If I were not Alexander I should have liked to be Diogenes."

The war which Philip had planned against Persia was only delayed two years by his death. In 334, Alexander invaded Asia Minor with about thirty-five thousand troops. Nearly half were Macedonians, the rest hired soldiers or troops sent by the Greek cities. The army took with it engineers for making bridges or siege towers, well diggers, surveyors to find out about routes and camp grounds, geographers to make maps, botanists and other learned men to collect specimens and find out more about the country they conquered. There was a baggage train, of course, and a military council of high officers trained by Philip. Everything was planned to go like clockwork.

Philip had merely meant to conquer Asia Minor. The Greek cities on the coast would be easily won over, and they would dry up the stream of hired soldiers on which the Persians relied. The great landowners of the country districts made splendid cavalry in the Persian style; but the peasants, though loyal to their lords and personally warlike, were too poor to afford the armor of Greek infantry. Hard fighting lay ahead of Alexander, but he was victorious.

After a while he found that he could not hold his gains without going further. Control of Asia Minor with its long seacoast depended on a fleet. The fleet of the Persians came from Egypt and the great Phoenician city of Tyre on the Syrian coast. Alexander advanced against Tyre because he had to, descending from mountainous country into the plain where Asia Minor borders on Syria.

Darius III, who had succeeded Artaxerxes, was a weak ruler, but he came of fighting stock and knew that he must battle for his kingdom. He could not, however, get together an army which was larger than the countryside would support. His native infantry was not equal to the Greeks, and his leadership was poor. When he met Alexander at the battle of the Issus, the Macedonian charged at the head of his men, while the Persian hovered in a chariot in the rear and speedily fled. Darius's leaderless men were cut to pieces, and Alexander found himself master of Syria.

He hurried to blockade Tyre, but found it difficult. The Tyrians kept his warships off by piling great boulders under water. Alexander sent merchant ships to haul these away, but the Tyrians ventured out in their own warships to attack them. Alexander brought up his fleet to protect his dredgers, but Tyrian divers cut their cables under water. Meanwhile, on the land side his engineers were unable for a long while to make the slightest progress. Tyre held out for seven months, but King Darius did not dare face Alexander again. Unaided, the city fell at last in July, 332. By November, Alexander was in Egypt, where he was received with joy, since the Egyptians had long desired to be free from the Persians. Alexander controlled the whole eastern end of the Mediterranean.

Once more his only defense lay in attack. The true center of the Persian empire lay across the Euphrates, in Media, Babylonia, and Persia. In Susa, long the capital, and in Persepolis, where the kings had built their palaces in the days of their pride, lay uncounted treasure piled up from the tribute of two hundred years. For this even Darius must fight. Eighteen months had gone by since his defeat, and he had by now refitted his forces. The cavalry, which had always been superb, was better armed. For the infantry

less could be done, seeing that to make new equipment took much time, and to drill fighters even longer. Darius was relying on chariots whose wheels had long knives sticking out. A few hundred of these might well be able to break up massed infantry if skillfully handled.

Darius gave battle on the flat plain of Gaugamela, since he was anxious to give his chariots a chance. There on the first of October, 331, Alexander found him. The chariots made their charge, but Alexander had screened his infantry by javelin men and slingers. For the sake of speed, the chariots had little armor. Men and

horses crashed to the ground, and very few of them reached the infantry. The rest of the battle swayed back and forth. The Persians had the greater numbers, but the Greeks the better army. They had a tradition of victory, too, and a finer commander.

Once more Darius took to flight. He might have spared himself the effort, for he had lost his kingdom by now and even his life. The Persian nobles whom he had twice deserted in battle were finished with him. He was arrested; and as the pursuit of Alexander came close, he was finally murdered.

There was now no king in the empire but Alexander. The men of Babylon came out to surrender. The satrap of Persia tried to keep him from entering his homeland but was swept aside. Alexander took Susa and Persepolis. He sat on the Great King's throne and seized his treasure. As a sign to the whole East, he set fire to the palace of King Xerxes and burned it to the ground. The miracle had come to pass. Greece had conquered the empire.

We need not follow Alexander farther east across the steppes of Turkestan, through the foothills of the Himalayas, into India. Susa had been only the center of an empire which stretched as far east as it did west. There were adventures ahead for Alexander with tribes, by lands and rivers which he had never heard of. But before he pursued his way, he had to face the problem of holding what he had won. It is what Alexander did to found an empire as much as his generalship that made him great.

Greeks generally thought that barbarians, which is what they called non-Greeks, were fit to be plundered or made slaves, rather than to rule. Alexander, however, was half barbarian himself; and he had seen the wonders of Babylonia and Egypt, as well as the splendor of Persian kings. He understood that East and West must be mingled into a greater whole and that he, Alexander, must have a share in both.

The first thing that he did was found many cities through the eastern world where homeless Greek soldiers found a new place to live and build their temples. Those cities acted as market places for country villages or stages on the trade routes which had run far in Persian times and were soon to be thronged with travelers. Alexandria in Egypt has always been the greatest of the towns that Alexander founded, but there were many others, including one called after Bucephalus, his horse. From these cities Greek ways spread all over the East. When the Romans came to rule two hundred years later, they found that Greek had become a second language through the eastern part of their whole empire. They were content to let it remain so and to speak it themselves; for the Romans, like the eastern peoples, had much to learn from the Greeks.

All this Alexander did, but in actually governing the peoples of the East he relied on themselves. He split up the power of the satraps, to be sure; and he left trusty Macedonian generals here and there with troops. All the same, he tried to employ the great Persian nobles, got to know them, dressed in eastern clothes himself, and liked his friends to do so. He married an eastern princess called Roxana and encouraged his friends to follow his example.

He did not want men to think of him as a conqueror, but rather as a godlike hero, born to rule. There is often something of this feeling about kingship. Philip's image had been carried in procession with those of the gods. Egyptian kings were thought divine, and the Persians could claim at least to be God's servants. Alexander had found these ideas in the East and was eager to adopt them because he needed loyalty. They meant something special to him, too. Achilles, his ancestor, was half divine. During the quarrels between his mother and Philip, Queen Olympias made a mystery of his birth, pretending that he was more than Philip's son. It is likely also that his victories had gone to his head. No one had ever done what he had done, and he was not yet thirty. Alexander gave out that he was not really Philip's son, but was born of a god.

It was a wise political stroke, but his Macedonian friends did not like it. They were many years away from home and they may have been tired of adventures. Perhaps they had their ambitions, too; and they did not wish Alexander to show favor to native princes. At all events, there were plots against him.

Alexander was noble and trusting by nature. Early in his campaigns his doctor was mixing a drink of medicine for him when a letter was brought in. He read it. It warned him that the doctor was planning to poison him. Alexander stretched out one hand for the drink, while with the other he offered the letter to his doctor. While the startled man read it, the king drained the medicine down.

After this, it is sad to discover that years later this very doctor took part in an attempt on Alexander's life. Alexander's new position was making him so lofty that he could trust no one.

The strain had begun to tell on him. If he made mistakes, his empire might collapse even more quickly than it had been won. At feasts he began to drink deeply, as his father had once done. His royal rages became terrible to endure. But victory followed him all the same wherever he went.

In 323, he was back from India in Babylon, preparing to conquer Arabia; but his amazing career was over at last. He fell sick of a fever and, weakened by battle wounds, could not throw it off. He died in the palace of the kings of Babylon on June 13, 323 B.C. He was only thirty-two years old and in the thirteenth year of his reign. He had conquered nearly all of the known world.

XVII

The New Age

after 323 B.C.

THE DEATH of Alexander ended an era. Greek history was now not so much Greek as the history of the mixed peoples of what we call the Middle East. The death of Alexander without an heir shaped the course of it. Queen Roxana was expecting a child and did soon bear a son, but an infant was useless in a time of such confusion. Alexander's generals were left to carve up his empire. Ptolemy seized Egypt. Antipater, who had long been regent in Macedon, laid claim to Greece. Seleucus set himself up in Babylon. After much fighting, these three men ruled separate kingdoms, all Greek and yet all native, Egyptian, Macedonian, and Asiatic.

Demosthenes in Athens had bided his time while Alexander lived, always urging the Athenians to strengthen themselves and hoping a chance might be given of breaking free. With the death of Alexander, his moment came. He toured the Peloponnese and roused the people to strike a blow for freedom. The Athenians at the head of an alliance defied Antipater, as their ancestors in earlier days had defied Xerxes.

History seldom repeats itself exactly. After a year of fighting, Antipater was victorious at the battle of Crannon. Athens was occupied by his troops and ceased to be a democracy. Demosthenes was condemned to die and fled for refuge to a famous temple of Poseidon. When his enemies caught up with him there, he was writing. He had poison concealed in the hollow reed which served him for a pen; and as they waited for him, he bit it. Thus died Demosthenes, an Athenian who would not accept the new age and led his people to fight for the freedom they had loved so long.

The world went on, and Greek culture did not perish. Indeed, as we have seen, it spread far wider than it had done before. It centered not on Athens, but on the new Egyptian city of Alexandria. By the change, it gained a wider outlook on the world. It lost, however, in quality. Alexandrian poets are charming rather than great. Greek art becomes more lifelike but less grand. Alexandrian scholars are men who collected the knowledge of the past instead of adding to it.

After a century and a half, or a little more, the Romans came to conquer Greece. They began to be active on all the borders of the Mediterranean. Everywhere they found a civilization ready to teach them much. The thoughts of the Greeks combined with the laws of the Romans have given us many of our own traditions. They were handed down to us through the Roman Empire.

Greek history, as we can see, was not over. Indeed, it still goes on today. After Alexander, however, we cannot study it alone, because it has merged with the history of many nations. Besides, for the next two thousand years, the Greeks were never in the old sense of the word a free people.

Greek Words and Proper Names

Note: The names marked with an asterisk (*) will appear again and again.

Chapter 1

*AEGEAN (E-*jee*-an) Sea in which lie the Greek islands

*PELOPONNESE (Pel-o-pon-*nese*) Southernmost part of Greece

PELOPS (*Pee*-lops) Hero after whom the Peloponnese is named

*ATHENS Greatest city of Greece

ZEUS Sky god and father of gods

POSEIDON (Po-*sy*-don) God of the sea

APOLLO (A-*pol*-lo) God of the sun

ARTEMIS (*Ar*-te-mis) Goddess of the moon

HERCULES (*Her*-cu-lees) Hero of Greek legend

*ACROPOLIS (A-*crop*-o-lis) Hill in the center of Athens

CECROPS (*Ke*-crops) First king of Athens

*PARTHENON (*Par*-the-non) Temple of Athene in Athens

Chapter II

ACHAEANS (A-*kee*-ans) Greeks of the times of early legends

DORIANS (*Dor*-i-ans) Later Greeks arriving about 1200 B.C.

ILIAD (*Il*-i-ad) Poem of Homer about the siege of Troy

HOMER Supposed author of *The Iliad* and *The Odyssey*

AGAMEMNON (A-ga-*mem*-non) Leader of the Greeks in *The Iliad*

MYCENAE (My-*see*-ne) City of Agamemnon, greatest king of the Achaeans

Odyssey (*Od*-is-sy) Poem of Homer about the voyage of Odysseus

ODYSSEUS (O-*diss*-seus) Hero of *Odyssey*

*MEDITERRANEAN (Me-di-ter-*rain*-e-an) Sea that borders Europe, Africa, and Asia

SCHLIEMANN (*Shlee*-man) Discoverer of ancient Troy and the ruins of Mycenae

HISSARLIK (*His*-sar-lik) Turkish name for the site of Old Troy

PRIAM (*Pry*-am) King of Troy

ARGOS (*Ar*-gos) Territory in the Peloponnese

NESTOR (*Nes*-tor) One of the heroes in *The Iliad*

Chapter III

CROESUS (*Kree*-sus) King of Lydia in Asia Minor

SOLON (*So*-lon) Wise man of Athens

TELLUS (*Tel*-lus) An Athenian

ELEUSIS (E-*leu*-sis) Place just outside Athens

CLEOBIS (*Cle*-o-bis) Young man of Argos

Greek Words and Proper Names

Bito (*Bit*-o) Young man of Argos
*Cyrus (*Sy*-rus) Founder of Persian empire
*Delphi (*Del*-fi) Site of a famous temple of Apollo
Herodotos (He-*rod*-o-tos) Greek historian
*Darius (Da-*ry*-us) Greatest Persian king

Chapter IV

Olympiad (O-*lim*-pi-ad) Period of four years between Olympic games
*Pheidippides (Fy-*dip*-id-ees) Famous Athenian runner
Theseus (*Thee*-seus) Famous Athenian king and hero
Pindar (*Pin*-dar) Greek poet
Pythian (games) (*Pith*-i-an) Adjective meaning "of Apollo"

Chapter V

*Aristodemos (*A*-ris-to-*deem*-os) A Spartan
Helot (*Hel*-lot) A Spartan serf, almost a slave

Chapter VI

*Darius (Da-*ry*-us) Greatest Persian king
Marathon (*Mar*-ra-thon) Battle where Athenians defeated Persians
Miltiades (Mil-*ty*-a-dees) Victorious general at Marathon
*Xerxes (*Zerk*-sees) Son of Darius
*Sardis (*Sar*-dis) Center of Persian government in Asia Minor; once capital of Croesus (Chap. III)
Hellespont (*Hel*-les-pont) Narrow sea separating Asia and Europe

*THERMOPYLAE (Ther-*mop*-i-le) Narrow pass where Spartans met Persians

LEONIDAS (Le-*on*-id-as) A king of Sparta (they had two kings, who did not rule but rather acted as generals)

Chapter VII

THEMISTOCLES (The-*mis*-to-klees) Athenian leader

TRIREME (*try*-reme) Greek warship

*ISTHMUS (*iss*-mus) A neck of land; *the* Isthmus is the one joining the Peloponnese to the rest of Greece

SALAMIS (*Sal*-a-mis) Naval battle in which Athenians and Greeks defeated Persians

SICINNUS (Si-*kin*-nus) Tutor to the children of Themistocles

Chapter VIII

*PERICLES (*Per*-i-klees) Athenian statesman who gave his name to the golden age.

Chapter IX

PIRAEUS (Py-*ree*-us) Port of Athens, about three miles away from it

EUPHRONIUS (Eu-*fro*-ni-us) Athenian vase painter and potter

PANAETIUS (Pan-*ee*-ti-us) Athenian vase painter in workshop of Euphronius

ONESIMUS (O-*nee*-si-mus) Athenian vase painter in workshop of Euphronius

Chapter X

*PARTHENON (*Par*-the-non) Temple of Athene at Athens

*ACROPOLIS (A-*crop*-o-lis) Hill in the center of Athens

*PHIDIAS (*Fid*-i-as) Great Athenian sculptor

Greek Words and Proper Names

Chapter XI

DIONYSUS (Dy-o-*ny*-sus) God of wine

*DIONYSIA (Dy-o-*nis*-i-a) Festival of Dionysus

BACCHUS (*Bak*-kus) Same as Dionysus

*AESCHYLUS (*Es*-ki-lus, or *Ees*-ki-lus) Oldest of three
    Athenian playwrights

*SOPHOCLES (*Sof*-o-klees) Second Athenian playwright

*EURIPIDES (Eu-*rip*-i-dees) Third Athenian playwright

PROMETHEUS (Pro-*mee*-theus) Enemy of Zeus in play of
    Aeschylus

HERMES (*Her*-mees) Messenger of Zeus

ARCHON (*ar*-kon) An Athenian official

CLYTEMNESTRA (Kly-tem-*nes*-tra) Wife of King Agamem-
    non (Chap. II) who murdered him

Chapter XII

*SOCRATES (*Sok*-ra-tees) Athenian wise man or philoso-
    pher

SOPHIST (*Soff*-ist) A wise man who taught for a fee

PHILOSOPHER (fi-*los*-o-fer) A wise man who tried to dis-
    cover truth in one of various ways

CRITIAS (*Kri*-ti-as) An Athenian dictator, onetime fol-
    lower of Socrates

ALCIBIADES (Al-ci-*by*-ad-es) Nephew of Pericles (see
    Chap. VIII) and onetime follower of Socrates

CRITO (*Kry*-to) Friend of Socrates

Chapter XIII

*PLATO (*Play*-to) Athenian philosopher

DION (*Dy*-on) Noble of Syracuse

SYRACUSE (*Sy*-ra-cuse) Greek city in Sicily

CARTHAGE (*Kar*-thage) Phoenician city in North Africa

DIONYSIUS (Dy-o-*nis*-i-us) Dictator of Syracuse

AEGINA (E-*jy*-na) Island near Athens and a rival of Athens

Chapter XIV

*XENOPHON (*Zen*-o-fon) Athenian adventurer and writer

*ARTAXERXES (Ar-tak-*zerk*-sees) Name of several Persian kings

CYRUS (*Sy*-rus) Pretender to Persian throne and namesake of founder of empire

TISSAPHERNES (Tiss-a-*fer*-nees) Persian nobleman

CLEARCHUS (Klee-*ar*-kus) Spartan general under Cyrus

*SARDIS (*Sar*-dis) (See Chap. VI) Center of Persian government in Asia Minor

SUSA (*Soo*-za) Persian capital beyond the Tigris river

EUPHRATES (Eu-*fray*-tees) One of the two chief rivers of Mesopotamia

THAPSACUS (*Thap*-sa-cus) Eastern city on the Euphrates

BABYLONIA (Bab-i-*lo*-ni-a) District in which Babylon, greatest city of Mesopotamia, was located

CUNAXA (Kew-*nax*-a) Battle in which Artaxerxes defeated Cyrus

TIGRIS (*Ty*-gris) Second of the chief rivers of Mesopotamia

GYMNIAS (*Jim*-ni-as) City on route to Black Sea

TREBIZOND (*Treb*-i-zond) Greek city on the Black Sea

Chapter XV

*PHILIP King of Macedon

*MACEDON *or* MACEDONIA (*Mas*-e-don, *Mas*-e-*don*-i-a) Kingdom in north of Greece

Greek Words and Proper Names

PERDICCAS (Per-*dik*-kas) Older brother of Philip

*ALEXANDER Oldest brother of Philip; also an earlier king still; also Alexander the Great, son of Philip

THEBES (*Theebs*) Greek city north of Athens

PHOCIANS (*Fo*-shi-ans) A Greek people living near Delphi

AMPHIPOLIS (Am-*fi*-pol-is) Greek town on the coast of Macedon

POTIDAEA (Pot-i-*dee*-a) Greek town on the coast of Macedon

*DEMOSTHENES (De-*mos*-the-nees) An Athenian statesman

PHILIPPICS (Fi-*lip*-pics) Speeches of Demosthenes against Philip

ISOCRATES (I-*sok*-ra-tees) An Athenian statesman

CHAERONEA (*Ker*-o-*ne*-a) A battle which made Philip master of Greece

DEMADES (*De*-ma-dees) An Athenian statesman

EPIRUS (E-*py*-rus) Kingdom bordering on Macedonia

Chapter XVI

OLYMPIAS (O-*limp*-i-as) Wife of Philip, mother of Alexander

BUCEPHALUS (Boo-*sef*-al-us) Alexander's horse

ARISTOTLE (*A*-ris-totle) Greek philosopher, pupil of Plato

AMYNTAS (A-*min*-tas) King of Macedon, father of Philip

DIOGENES (Dy-*oj*-e-nees) Greek philosopher living in Corinth

CORINTH (*Kor*-inth) Greek city at the Isthmus (Chap. VII)

PHOENICIAN (Fe-*nish*-i-an) Adjective describing an Asiatic race which built the great trading cities of Tyre and Carthage (Chap. XIII)

Issus (*Iss*-us) River in Syria, site of Alexander's first victory over the Persian king

Gaugamela (Gau-ga-*mee*-la) Site of Alexander's second victory over the Persian emperor

Tyre Greatest Phoenician city on coast of Syria

Persepolis (Per-*sep*-o-lis) One of the capitals of the Persian kings

Alexandria (A-lex-*an*-dri-a) Greatest city founded by Alexander

Roxana (Rox-*an*-a) Queen of Alexander

Chapter XVII

Ptolemy (*Tol*-e-mi) General of Alexander, later king of Egypt

Antipater (*An*-ti-pay-ter) General of Alexander, regent of Macedon and later king

Seleucus (Se-*lew*-cus) General of Alexander, later king in Asia

Crannon (*Cran*-non) Town in Thessaly where Antipater won victory over Greeks

Index

Index

Index

ABOUT THE AUTHOR

Olivia Coolidge was born and educated in England. Her father was Sir Robert Ensor, a well-known journalist and historian who loved the classics and wanted his children to study them. Mrs. Coolidge did not like studying Greek until one winter when she happened to sprain her ankle. During her three months' convalescence, she discovered the magic of Greek poetry. Her enthusiasm continued and a few years later she won a scholarship to Oxford University to study the classics.

After coming to the United States, Mrs. Coolidge taught English for several years and also started her writing career. She is the author of eighteen books, including *Men of Athens* and *The King of Men*. Greek history has always been one of her favorite fields and she has enjoyed traveling in Greece and visiting the ancient ruins there.

Olivia Coolidge and her husband live in Cambridge, Maryland. They have four children and thirteen grandchildren.

ABOUT THE ILLUSTRATOR

Enrico Arno has had a distinguished career as an illustrator of children's books. He was born in Mannheim, Germany, and educated in Berlin. He emigrated to Italy in 1940, working for Mondrian in Milan and later for a publisher in Rome. Mr. Arno came to the United States in 1947. He and his wife live in Sea Cliff, New York.